Born in Dewsbury, Yorkshire, *Andrew Morton* is 29 and was educated in Leeds and at Sussex University, Brighton where he studied history.

He joined the *Daily Express* in 1978 where he worked as a sub-editor before joining the *Daily Star*. Since joining the *Star* he has worked as a sub-editor and reporter and is currently the paper's royal correspondent, following the royal family around the world.

Mick Seamark is 30, and was born in Buckinghamshire. He joined the *Daily Star* when the newspaper was launched in 1978 and has reported stories at home and abroad. In April 1982 he sailed from Portsmouth to cover the Falklands War, reporting the fighting at sea and on the Falklands, and walked into Port Stanley minutes after Argentina surrendered.

Andrew
The Playboy Prince

Andrew Morton and Mick Seamark

SEVERN HOUSE

This first U.K. hardcover edition published 1983 by
SEVERN HOUSE PUBLISHERS LTD of
4 Brook Street, London W1Y 1AA
with acknowledgement to Transworld Publishers Ltd

ISBN 0 7278 0988 1

Printed and bound in Great Britain by
Anchor Brendon Ltd, Tiptree, Essex

Contents

Andrew
The Playboy Prince

1 *Andymania*

It was a cold and windy November evening. Hardly a night to spend standing around. But the street corner chestnut sellers were doing a roaring trade as a crowd of several thousand gathered in busy Regent Street in the heart of London's shopping centre.

The crowd, mainly of housewives on their way home from Christmas shopping and young office girls, waited patiently for a glimpse of one young man . . . Prince Andrew, the third-in-line to the throne. He was due to switch on the famous Regent Street lights, a ceremony his sister-in-law, Princess Diana, had performed the year before. He didn't disappoint them. When he pulled up in his black Rolls Royce after a short journey from his flat in Buckingham Palace the waiting throng let out a roar of greeting. Dozens of young girls squealed with delight when they saw the hero whose picture adorned their office and bedroom walls.

It was only Andrew's second public speaking engagement, and the first time he had had to endure the ordeal of speaking live in front of the TV cameras. If he was nervous it didn't show. He waved and grinned broadly and wagged his finger in mock disapproval saying: 'I heard that' when a voice from the crowd piped up: 'Kooee' in reference to his much publicised relationship with actress Koo Stark. The scene was set for one of those good humoured and informal royal occasions that are the hallmark of the modern British monarchy. As the evening wore on it became much more than that.

He left the crowd waiting while he went into the fashion store Jaeger which was being used as the venue for the switching on ceremony. But before he could meet his public again he had to bow to the tyranny of TV. Their schedules meant that the Prince had to wait ten minutes before he could make his short speech. He filled in the time chatting amiably to a group of shopgirls.

He joked with them about their working hours, curiously asked if any of them could do first aid and wondered what on earth were 'separates'. He also gave an insight into his own life when he revealed that he couldn't spare a lot of time to go shopping as much as he would like. He hinted that his family had 'special problems' – an oblique reference to the fact that his shopping sprees would be dogged by photographers.

The waiting over, Andrew walked smartly out onto the second floor balcony. He was now on parade. The cheering was louder, the screams shriller. People below craned their necks to get a better view as Andrew launched into his first televised speech. He talked about the royal link with Christmas trees and before switching on said that he hoped the 55,000 light bulbs adorning the trees would work. Even though his speech was rather routine the crowd loved every minute. They gave a huge roar when the eleven rows of Christmas tree lights which criss-crossed Regent Street bathed them in light. Andrew too lapped up the limelight, waving and grinning broadly. Apart from his younger brother Edward he is the least experienced of the royals but he clearly enjoyed his chance to shine. For most of his working life the young helicopter pilot is with his squadron at Culdrose in Cornwall. Although he prefers to keep partly in the shadows no-one loves the cheers of the crowd more than Andrew. But he ignored the cries of 'More, more' and gave a final cheery wave before once more walking inside for a reception with showbiz personalities. While he chatted with squeaky voiced actress Bonnie Langford and BBC newsreader Jan Leeming the crowd chanted: 'We want Andy' and ignored a police inspector who used a loudhailer in a vain attempt to get Andrew's fan club to move in order to clear a path for the traffic which by now had formed a jam of epic proportions.

Girls started screaming in anticipation if anyone so much as went near the balcony. Near hysteria gripped the tightly-packed throng. Several girls fainted and had to be passed over the heads of others before they reached the safety of the crash barriers. Shaken and bemused, they were comforted by policewomen who normally expect this kind of behaviour at pop concerts. When Andrew finally emerged on the street the crowd went wild. Andymania had hit Britain.

Lines of police linked arms in a desperate attempt to keep the cheering crowd from Andrew. As he climbed into his car he looked rather apprehensive, as well he might. The crowd pushed and shoved forward, bobbies' helmets were knocked off, the thin blue line bulging and snaking under the pressure. It took a couple of minutes before they could restore enough order to allow Andrew to drive off into the night. The astonished manager of Jaeger, Mike Morton, watched the scenes of mayhem from the same balcony where Andrew had made his speech a few minutes earlier.

'It's absolutely amazing,' he said with obvious bewilderment. 'I've not seen anything like this since the days of Beatlemania.' And it certainly is amazing. Royals generate applause and cheers, not chanting and screams. The young helicopter pilot, just coming up to his twenty-third birthday, has captured the heart of the nation. But what is it about Andrew that sparks a response that would be unthinkable were it to happen to his elder brother Charles or sister Anne? He has always held a special place in his mother's heart; now it seems the same is true for the nation. Is it his cheerful charm, his naturalness, his exploits as a helicopter pilot in the Falklands or his roguish reputation with beautiful girls? Or a combination of these that got to make Andrew the most charismatic of the young royals? His arrival on the scene has given a new meaning to the initials HRH. With Andrew they stand for His Royal Heartthrob. . . .

2 *The Boss*

On a chill February afternoon the young man Prince Philip called 'The Boss' came bouncing into the world. Andrew Albert Christian Edward Mountbatten Windsor was born on February 19th, 1960. He was a few hours late – but none the less welcome for that. His arrival heralded the start of the Queen's second family – a source of great joy and pleasure to her.

She had always promised that she would have a large family but the premature death of her father, King George VI, in 1952 meant that the private pleasures of family life were curtailed by the cares of monarchy. The fact that there was a gap of ten years between elder sister Anne and Andrew showed just how long that regal apprenticeship was. Now she was happy to leave the august affairs of State for a while and concentrate once more on being a mother. Even so it was difficult to break free completely.

Hours after Andrew was born in the Belgian Room at Buckingham Palace, she was sitting up in bed reading through the papers in her red State 'boxes', a vase of white rose and carnations from Prince Philip by her bedside.

Andrew was the first boy to be born to a

reigning monarch since 1857 when Queen Victoria gave birth to her youngest child, Princess Beatrice. Andrew also ousted Anne from her position as second-in-line to the throne. He took over the Number Two spot by virtue of the fact that he was a boy. Women's liberation has not yet reached the lofty heights of royal succession.

From the start Andrew's parents decided that he should be brought up as 'normally' as possible. Normal that is by royal standards. They felt that he should escape the glare of publicity that had surrounded and threatened to swamp Charles and Anne. In fact he was so seldom seen in public that rumours circulated that all was not well with the Queen's third child.

The veil of secrecy which the Queen deliberately drew over Andrew even extended to the announcement of her pregnancy. The Queen faced the longest tour of her reign – a nine week cross-country circuit of Canada – when she discovered that she was expecting. When she informed Canada's Prime Minister John Diefenbaker he gallantly offered to cut short the tour. Characteristically she refused for she was acutely conscious of all the intense planning which had gone into the tour – planning which took no account of her delicate condition.

Preparations for royal tours are indeed elaborate. A 6,000 word letter from the Queen's private secretary goes out to the host nation listing her requirements. As she likes to fit as much into her timetable as possible the Queen does not welcome the idea of long lunches – fifty minutes is the limit. But in the early stages of pregnancy she came to regret a tight schedule which left her scant time to relax.

She watched her diet even more closely than normal. Oysters, lobsters and other shellfish were taboo while she was travelling. The Queen is not fussy about her food; what she eats is more a matter of prudence than taste. Even so, to be on the safe side, she cut out the one glass of wine she normally permits herself and kept rigidly to the Malvern water which goes with her on every trip abroad. No doubt the expectant mother allowed herself one little indulgence - her love of chocolate mints.

In spite of these precautions the gruelling tour took its toll and newspapers reported that she looked 'tired' and 'drawn'. She ignored the advice of her physician to go to bed and rest for a few days. Eventually her body rebelled and she was forced to cancel a planned visit to Dawson City. Buckingham Palace officials trotted out the excuse of 'tiredness' as a convenient smokescreen.

In the end she resumed her gruelling tour timetable but when she arrived back at Buckingham Palace she had a welcoming party of two top royal doctors who took one look at the pale and tired thirty-three-year-old mother and ordered her to bed for complete rest and quiet. Five days later she travelled to Balmoral, her Highland summer retreat, and it was only then that the public were let in on the secret she had been nursing. A terse announcement from the Palace said: 'The Queen will not be undertaking any more public engagements in the foreseeable future.' Her private secretary Commander Richard Colville added gallantly: 'The Queen and Prince Philip have always been anxious to have more children and are very happy about it.' The public were astonished, having grown used to a young Queen with two growing children. However, once the news sunk in messages of congratulation, not to mention bootees and blankets, flooded in by the sackful to Buckingham Palace. While the Queen took it easy, forsaking her horse-riding and going for daily walks with her corgis instead, magazines were full of advice on bringing up baby.

Right up to the morning of the birth she tried to keep to her regular routine – although she did miss the State opening of Parliament. Normally she is up around 8.00 and minutes afterwards her personal maid Margaret MacDonald – known affectionately as Bobo – brings in a pot of tea. Since 1949 the Queen and Prince Philip have slept in separate though adjoining bedrooms and each morning he joins her over breakfast to listen to the BBC and flick through the morning papers. Like her sister, Elizabeth is something of a wizard when it comes to solving crosswords and as she pondered over 'One across' she would chat to her children. Both Charles and Anne wanted a new baby boy – Anne so that she could have someone to go riding with. When this private 'family time' is over she is joined by her private secretaries.

They help her deal with correspondence related to her job – invitations to open factories, speak at dinners and so on. Then she turns her attention to the red, green, black or blue State 'boxes' which arrive each day for her attention. They contain top secret background from the

Foreign Office about events making the headlines, Government acts for her signature, Home Office papers and lists of appointees - a new Minister perhaps - to approve. Ironically, although the Queen has little political power, she is the one person living who has seen the most vital documents - secret or otherwise - which impinge on the welfare of the State. She has seen eight Prime Ministers come and go and been privy to the highest matters of Government. As incoming Prime Ministers have found to their cost, her opinions and advice are not to be taken lightly.

Her daily State work over, she attends any formal engagements she may have. If the rest of her day is free she generally spends time with her young children, playing card games or simply reading stories. It was into this atmosphere, a curious mixture of formality and levity, that Andrew arrived at 3.30 on the afternoon of February 19th. The white-haired midwife Sister Rowe, who had been present at the birth of Charles and Anne, and four doctors, lead by Welshman Lord Evans, ensured a safe delivery. He weighed in at seven pounds three ounces, an average size, but slightly lighter than elder brother Charles. When the traditional announcement of the birth was posted on the railings of Buckingham Palace a huge cheer rang out from the crowd who had been waiting patiently since early morning for news. It said simply: 'The Queen was safely delivered of a son at 3.30 pm today. Her Majesty and the Infant Prince are both doing well.' When the Queen felt well enough, groups of Palace servants, who had chipped in sixpence a time for a bouquet of flowers, were ushered in to see the baby by Sister Rowe.

While tug sirens wailed, salutes were fired and RAF Arrows staged a spectacular flypast over London, there was one significant fact missing from the national celebrations – what to call the infant Prince?

The surname had already been arrived at – Mountbatten Windsor. This was a departure from the surname of Charles and Anne. For in royal circles even the naming of parts takes on a complexity mere mortals never dream of. After her father's death, the Queen decided to keep the family name of Windsor. This move followed considered advice from the then Prime Minister Winston Churchill. A royal decree duly followed. But it left Prince Philip in an ambiguous position as his children would not bear his surname. This was resolved in a typical British compromise when another royal decree announced that Andrew would be named Mountbatten Windsor. A neat solution but one which did not help the thousands of wellwishers who wanted to raise their glasses and drink a toast to the baby. 'Prince Who?' was the cry. After an agony of selection the couple arrived on names which honoured each family's traditions. Andrew was chosen in memory of Prince Philip's cavalry officer father. Albert to remember beloved Bertie, the Queen's father, and Christian echoed Philip's Danish ancestry. King Christian IX of Denmark was the baby's great-great-grandfather while Edward matched the relationship on the Queen's side. King Edward VII was Andrew's great-great-grandfather.

But Andrew wasn't the only one to hog the

headlines. A week later Princess Margaret announced her engagement to Anthony Armstrong Jones, later Lord Snowdon. Again the news came as a shock to the public. When he was in the presence of the royal-family it was assumed that he was there in his profession as a photographer, not as a suitor. Andrew soon had company, for the early Sixties proved to be something of a boom time for the royal family. In June 1960 the Duke and Duchess of Kent were married and a year later their first son, George, Earl of St Andrews was born.

Their daughter Lady Helen Windsor came along in 1964. Just eighteen months after her wedding in May Princess Margaret gave birth to a son, David, Viscount Linley, and in May 1964 a daughter, Sarah Frances Elizabeth. Princess Alexandra and Angus Ogilvy, who were married in 1963, had a son James in 1964 and a daughter, Marina, in 1966. Before that the Queen rounded off her family with Edward who was born on March 10th 1964. Although the succession was now well and truly assured the Queen began to come under fire for the very stable family life she had established. As the Sixties started to swing the Queen was seen as something of a throwback to an earlier era, an age whose values and traditions the angry young men of the time were busily discarding. Her traditional and rather staid lifestyle compared unfavourably with the stylish Jacqueline Kennedy and Grace Kelly, the elegant and chic Princess of Monaco.

The Queen took little or no notice of the criticism and simply got on with enjoying life as a mother. She and Prince Philip had firmly decided that Andrew should not be in the public eye quite so much as Anne and Charles. They felt the excessive publicity had had a harmful effect, particularly on Prince Charles who was by nature a shy youngster.

When he first went to Cheam preparatory school he found it virtually impossible to push his way through to the school gates such was the crush of people waiting to see him. Princess Anne had suffered too. She nearly ended up in tears when she was taken to a fairground during a holiday in France. Far from enjoying the fun of the fair she became the focus of the fans and had to make something of a hasty exit. It is because the royals are constantly in the spotlight that they place such a premium on their privacy. For this reason Elizabeth felt it wise to let Andrew grow in the shadows.

Just a month after he was born, royal photographer Cecil Beaton took Andrew's official photograph in his wicker cot in the Buckingham Palace nursery. After that there was a complete news ban for six months. All the Queen's Press Secretary would reveal was that Andrew had blue eyes and didn't cry much. Hardly the sort of material to fuel the engines of curiosity for long. The adoring public got a brief glimpse of the infant when, as an afterthought, the Queen gave permission for him to be pictured for a very special occasion – the Queen Mother's sixtieth birthday celebration at Clarence House.

Then the shutters came down again and it wasn't until he was sixteen months old that he was again seen, this time in the arms of his mother, snuggling against her bright scarlet tunic at the Trooping of the Colour ceremony. When he pointed at a flight of sixteen Javelin aircraft roaring overhead in salute, the rumours that he was somehow abnormal were instantly silenced.

However the incident illustrates the tightrope the monarchy walks. If you reveal nothing about life inside the royal circle, then ill-informed gossip flows in to the vacuum. If you show too much then the mystique of the monarchy is undermined. It is rather like a perpetual Dance of the Seven Veils, revealing just enough to keep the public interested but keeping the essentials away from prying eyes.

Although he could escape the cameras Andrew couldn't evade the bureaucrats. Like every other baby he had to be registered. And to show that civil servants are even-handed in their approach, when Prince Philip came to register Andrew's birth, like everyone else, he was given a standard form from the National Health Service stating that he was entitled to claim for orange juice, cheap milk and vitamins. And to drive the proletarian point home the entry for Andrew – number 194 – followed that of a baby boy born to a labourer and his wife.

Andrew was christened soon afterwards in the airy Music Room at Buckingham Palace. Unlike the christenings of his brother and sister no Press were allowed. It was a small family affair. His godparents were Lord Elphinstone, the Earl of Euston, Princess Alexandra, the Duke of Gloucester and Mrs Harold Phillips – all close personal friends.

Like his ancestors, Andrew was swaddled in a christening robe of Honiton lace and the gold lily font containing Jordan water was brought from Windsor Castle for the occasion. It has been used for every christening since 1840.

If Andrew was a mystery to the public, to his adoring nanny Mabel Anderson he was a night and day responsibility. It was a burden she did not take lightly. 'Our Mabel', as she is affectionately known by the royal family, is the Rolls Royce of the nanny world. She runs her nursery with smooth efficiency and the only sound you will hear from her is the clicking of her tongue when one of her charges steers the wrong course. Andrew, nicknamed Baby Grumpling because of his bad temper, led her a merry dance.

This Mary Poppins character has been with the royal family for more than thirty years and is currently employed by the Prince and Princess of Wales as the housekeeper at their Highgrove home. But no doubt she gives the odd hint to Prince William's nanny, Barbara Barnes, about nursery routine. She has had plenty of experience, seeing two generations of Windsors reach maturity.

A policeman's daughter from Bootle in Lancashire and educated at the local grammar school, Mabel's one ambition in life was to look after children. Even as a teenage student at the local technical college where she studied domestic science she earned a reputation as the best babysitter in town.

When her father was killed during the Blitz she returned to her mother's old home in Elgin, forty miles from Balmoral. The first job of this quiet, softly-spoken young girl was with a South African family living in Scotland who had two young boys who needed taking care of. By all accounts the slimly-built young lady was a roaring success, spinning the youngsters fairy stories and taking them off to the kitchen to make gingerbread men for a treat. When the family went back to South Africa she advertised for a new job in the Lady magazine. By chance Princess Elizabeth saw the advert and asked Mabel to come for an interview. It was clear from the outset that this quiet but firm young woman was the one to look after her children. Mabel was hired.

When Andrew was born it was as though Mabel had been given a new lease of life. Anne and Charles had long outgrown nursery days and Mabel was thinking of moving on. It was not to be. She showed her devotion to her new charge by refusing to take a day off from work for five months after Andrew was born. She rarely took an evening off, preferring instead to watch the TV in the Palace day nursery with a microphone linked to the night nursery where Andrew slept. If he ever had nightmares or woke with earache it was Mabel who comforted Andrew, made him a hot cup of cocoa, and tucked him back in bed.

So closely did she guard her charge that when Prince Philip and the Queen went to Windsor for weekends they left baby Andrew behind rather than disturb the nursery routine. Four years later she showed the same intense devotion to Edward. When the youngster was rushed to Great Ormond Street Children's hospital with suspected appendicitis old Mabel went with him and slept in the next room. As it was Christmas she was thoughtful enough to bring along a bright red stocking filled with goodies.

She saw to it that Andrew's socks were darned, his shoes cleaned and his clothes replaced. She made sure he ate his breakfast porridge and finished his bread and butter at teatime. Mabel was a full time guardian angel who also had a bit of fun with her charges. She never hit or spanked Andrew, preferring instead to use her authority and personality to instill obedience. Like Charles and Anne before him, it was Mabel who taught Andrew how to play hopscotch, press flowers from the Palace gardens beneath the pages of heavy telephone directories and praised his early attempts to draw and paint.

She even invented counting games for the toddler to play. The nursery at Buckingham Palace is in the north-east corner overlooking the Mall. Mabel would lift Andrew up to the window and make him count horses, taxis or buses or even how many strides the scarlet-coated soldier on sentry duty took.

Andrew had his own little spade, fork and rake to take with him when he went out to play in the Palace gardens. But he would often uproot as many flowers as weeds on his excursions. Most of his nursery toys were hand-me-downs from his brother and sister. But a pink rocking elephant made by Prince Charles took pride of place in the toddler's nursery.

On fine days Andrew played a novel game of hide and seek with Mabel. She used Andrew's favourite corgi dogs, Sherry and Whisky, spending several months training them to hide in the bushes and trees in the gardens. On her word of command they would go running off and after counting to ten she and the infant would go and search for them. But the thing she is best remembered for by the royal children is her uncanny ability to weave magic with words. She kept Andrew entranced for hours with bedtime stories of elves, wizards and fairies. When Prince Charles wrote his children's book, *The Old Man of Lochnagar*, he said that he owed his technique of spinning a good yarn to Nanny Anderson.

In spite of the relaxation of protocol over the years Andrew was still dressed twice a day in clean clothes before he was presented to his mother. His pure cotton and wool suits required careful cleaning and ironing by the meticulous Mabel. These days attitudes have changed within the royal family. At Gatcombe Park in Gloucestershire, the home of Princess Anne and Captain Mark Phillips, the routine is more relaxed. Young Peter runs in and out of the living room at will and the room itself often looks more like a playground than a Princess's parlour.

Although Nanny Anderson was a constant companion, Andrew's mother also had more time for her young son. She had mastered the intricacies of statecraft, the daily boxes from Downing Street and the Foreign Office holding few terrors or surprises. It was time to go on to automatic pilot and relax a little. Andrew would sit near her and play while she pored over State papers at her highly-polished table. Visitors, bracing themselves for an interview with the monarch, would often be astonished to find her on the floor playing games with the toddler.

On fine days they went for walks in the royal gardens or she would watch him play in the sandpit or on the climbing frame which was specially built for him. It was his mother, and not Mrs Anderson, who taught Andrew the alphabet and the Queen looked forward to Mabel's night off with relish. For then she could go to the nursery and bath and read bedtime stories to her favourite son. She had a miniature blackboard and wooden clock installed in the dining room so that she could teach him how to tell the time and count. It was in this stimulating and caring atmosphere that the boy who was a heartbeat away from the throne grew up.

But the life of a young royal did have its drawbacks. His mother and father were away for his first birthday, touring India, Pakistan and Nepal. They missed his third birthday, this time on a trip to Australia. But they rang his sister Anne and asked her to make sure he had a happy birthday. However they were present to watch him blow out the four candles on his cake a year later.

Even though Andrew was not constantly by his parents' side he still had to master the rudiments of royal protocol. All servants were addressed as 'Mister', a formality which he applies to this day. The toddler had a special joint name for Nanny Anderson and his mother – Mamba. By the time he was four he had mastered the old-fashioned custom of kissing his mother's and grandmother's hand each time they met.

However, he was spared the finer points of etiquette which his mother and Princess Margaret had had to master. When they were youngsters their mother, then the Duchess of York, played an etiquette game which taught them how to address people properly. It went something like this . . .

'Now,' said the Duchess. 'Imagine I'm the Prime Minister.'

'Good morning, Mrs Baldwin,' said Princess Elizabeth.

'And this time,' continued the Duchess, 'I'm the Archbishop of Canterbury.'

'Good morning, Your Grace,' came the sweet reply from Margaret Rose.

Besides the basics of royal etiquette Andrew also set about learning some of the social graces that are essential in the world of the aristocracy. When he was little more than two years old he was given his first ride on a Shetland pony, clip-clopping along in front of Princess Anne and the Queen in the Royal Mews. As he grew bigger so did his horses, graduating from a half Shetland called Valkyrie to another called Mister Dinkum and then to a gentle polo pony called Zamba.

Although a competent horseman, Andrew is no match for his sister and it is the female side of the family where horses are taken most seriously. The Queen owns a string of fine thoroughbreds and both she and the Queen Mother are keen race-goers. But some of his comments reveal that he does not quite share their enthusiasm. During a visit to Cowes he joined one group of ladies who were discussing the merits of various hunters. Andrew screwed up his face in mock contempt and said: 'Horses, bloody horses. I'm sick of hearing about them. Can't you talk about anything else?'

He was taught to swim in the Palace pool by his father and later went to weekly swimming lessons at a Mayfair pool with cousin David, Viscount Linley and brother Edward. And

Madame Vacani, who taught Charles and Anne how to dance, was brought in to tutor the young Prince in the rudiments of ballroom technique. It didn't equip him for the disco if one of his former partners is to be believed. She said: 'As a dancer he is only so-so. He has little experience of disco music which is not surprising as he says he was brought up to do Highland reels and the waltz.'

The Queen Mother commissioned the world-renowned sculptress Franta Belsky to do a bronze head of Andrew before he lost his chubby baby looks. During the eight sittings she came to the conclusion that Andrew had his father's head and colouring but his mother's mouth and nose. He even aped his father's actions. When he was a toddler it was the family custom for the ladies to go by car to the church at Sandringham and the men to walk across the common. Andrew demanded to go with papa, rather than sit in the car. He got his own way and strolled across the park with his hands behind his back à la Philip. Even at two he was confident enough to shake hands with the head of British Rail's Eastern Region on the way back from Sandringham and later he gave a shy wave to the crowds at Windsor.

Like his parents he had a love of innocent – and some not so innocent – practical jokes, proof of his confident and extrovert nature. When a foot man was laying the table he was momentarily mystified when all the knives and forks went missing. He needn't have wondered. There was Andrew hiding underneath the table and taking them as he went by. On another occasion he sneaked up behind a sentry and silently tied his shoelaces together. As sentries on guard duty are not allowed to move they had to grimace and bear it. It was 'that young imp' who took a radio in the nursery to bits and caused consternation when he went missing – only to be found fast asleep in the airing cupboard when he became bored with his game of hide and seek.

When bubble bath was poured into the heated Palace pool it was Andrew who was held to blame. It was Andrew who broke the greenhouse windows with a football. 'He will make a good footballer, I'm sure,' said his doting grandmother proudly. And woe betide any footman who got in his way when he raced up and down the long, red-carpeted corridors in his toy car or flew down the stairs using a tea tray as a makeshift sledge.

The same love of mischief had prompted his mother to walk backwards and forwards in front of the guard at Buckingham Palace to see how often he would present arms. Three years later as a bored schoolgirl she tipped an inkwell over her head to relieve a tedious lesson in Latin grammar.

When he was older he spent long hours whizzing up and down the fire escape harness at Sandringham. It took only seven seconds to reach the ground from his first floor bedroom twenty-one feet above. After each descent he would scamper up for another go . . . and another . . . and another. He used it so often that the cable on the harness had to be repaired. But he endeared himself to the world when he decided to prick the pomp and circumstance at a colour ceremony.

When the 1st Battalion Gordon Highlanders

paraded before Balmoral Castle to receive new colours from the Queen, young Andrew was in a mischievous mood. As royal guard commander Major Nigel Oxley marched smartly forward and asked the Queen: 'Permission to march off the old colours, Ma'am,' Andrew leaned forward and said to his grandmother in a loud stage whisper: 'I do wish mummy would say "No" sometimes.'

His boisterous spirit had the occasional unfortunate result. Like the time he was playing with his father in a mock bedtime boxing match. During the horseplay one of his right hooks got through and left Prince Philip with a real shiner that even the application of raw steak could not disguise. He was due at a film première that night and as he stepped out of the car he pointed to his black eye and said ruefully: 'That was the Boss.' His tendency to dominate could spill over into bossiness, a characteristic mixing with children his own age would subdue. The last thing the Queen wanted was her son to grow up as an 'only child'. The arrival of Edward meant he had someone to share his games with and the royal population explosion in the early Sixties gave Andrew plenty of playmates. One of his early chums was a certain Lady Diana Spencer whom he met when he was at Sandringham. As a youngster she always said that she was going to marry Andrew. Right family, wrong name. Unlike his mother who watched the world go by with envy through the Palace railings, Andrew was more fortunate. When he started his first formal lessons under governess Katherine Peebles in the schoolroom at Buckingham Palace he had two boys and two girls for company. Justin Beaumont,

James Steel, Victoria Butler, the daughter of Lord Dunboyne, and Katie Seymour daily joined Andrew for lessons in maths, geography and reading. They used the revolutionary forty-four word alphabet but the Queen confessed to one teacher during a visit that it hadn't worked wonders with Andrew. 'He's behind in his reading,' she told him.

Their geography lessons were made more interesting when he traced his mother's tour around various Caribbean islands by sticking pins and coloured cotton on a large scale map of the world. Later the foursome were joined by David, Viscount Linley. It wasn't all work at Britain's most exclusive class. They enjoyed days out together, once travelling across London to visit the Blue Peter and Playschool studios and see how their favourite programmes were produced.

But while french and piano lessons were added to the daily routine the excitement of the week was when a small bus entered the gates of Buckingham Palace containing youngsters from the 1st Marylebone Cub pack. The troop – named the Fighting First because so many of their members were killed in the First World War – played games like 'bulldogs' which involved lots of rough and tumble. Andrew learned about woodcraft, played soccer and was taught how to identify various wild birds and flowers.

His experience was further broadened by visits to a local gym and soccer pitch. In keeping with his parents' wishes the trips were veiled in secrecy.

But he couldn't be kept in the shade forever. The growing young boy needed room to develop . . . it was time he went to school.

3 *Action Man Two*

Most people in Britain accept universal education as a fact of life. So it is something of a surprise to discover that Andrew was only the second son of a monarch to enjoy this privilege. Charles was the first to venture outside the Palace walls and face his contemporaries in the hurly burly of classroom life. Other royals, including the Queen and Princess Margaret, had had to be content with private tuition within the Palace gates. Other princes had been to university, none to an ordinary school.

At the age of eight-and-a-half Andrew took his first steps into Heatherdown, an Ascot preparatory school near to Windsor Castle, the Queen's weekend retreat. Throughout his school career and beyond, inevitable and sometimes unfair comparisons have been made between Andrew and his elder brother. To Andrew's obvious chagrin he found that whatever his achievements, be it in acting, swimming, or sailing, Charles had done it first and usually done it better. The fact that Andrew often aped his brother's antics earned him the nickname Action Man Two, not a title he was particularly fond of.

But the similarity in their education disguises the differences in their personalities. Whereas

Charles was a shy, thoughtful boy, often the butt of abuse and the victim of bullies, Andrew was more suited to the brawling behaviour of his school-chums. Extrovert, cocky almost, full of bounce and confidence way beyond his years Andrew was prepared to give as good as he got and stand up for himself. When Charles first went to Cheam prep school he was hounded by inquisitive members of the public and Press eager to find out as much as they could about the curious phenomenon of an heir to the throne going to a 'normal' school. He had an unhappy time there, finding the transition from the quiet ordered life of the Palace nursery to the shouting, screaming, pushing way of strife in an all-boys school too much to take. Andrew was quite another kettle of fish.

He loved mixing with youngsters his own age and was treated exactly as any other new pupil. He wore the same grey uniform, red cap and tie and shared a dormitory with six other youngsters in Tempest House. Soon after he arrived with his mother and father, the pipe-smoking headmaster James Edwards gave the new boys a short pep talk. 'I told them not to put too many conkers in their pockets – that sort of thing,' he said.

He was up at 7.15 each day and studied everything from scripture to maths – the usual array of lessons you will find at any junior school. In the afternoon the youngsters had a chance to let off steam in games of soccer or rugby in the school's thirty acres of grounds.

His mother heaved a sigh of relief when she learned that television watching was strictly limited. There had been tears earlier when Andrew, whose favourite programme was *Champion the*

Wonder Horse, was told that he was in danger of becoming a TV addict and ordered to watch less and read more. When he first arrived at the school he complained to matron that he had to go to bed too early. 'All the best programmes come on after we've gone to sleep. I'm allowed to watch them at home,' he said petulantly.

Although the whole emphasis of Andrew's upbringing was to make it as normal as possible, the young boy enjoyed more thrills and privileges because of his position than anyone else of that age. He and Edward were taken along to Lords cricket ground in London and taught how to use a bat by cricket veteran Len Muncer. The MCC Secretary Billy Griffiths took a long look at the youngster and pronounced: 'He might make a very good bowler.' Former tennis champion and now BBC commentator Dan Maskell gave him regular hour-long tennis coaching during secret visits to Wimbledon and he also went to weekly ice skating lessons at a rink in Richmond. He was put through his paces by Roy Lee, who confessed he felt 'sick' when asked to coach the Queen's son. Andrew had the rink all to himself as fellow skaters were cleared off the ice by security staff before he arrived. 'Security' was the excuse given but it demonstrates just how far removed Andrew was from leading a normal life.

Indeed what youngster could boast that he had been taught how to fish for salmon by the Queen Mother or gone for impromptu driving lessons with ex-world-champion racing driver Graham Hill? What other boy could boast a gift of a £4,000 version of the Aston Martin used in the James Bond movie *Goldfinger*? Andrew could, although the Queen banned the super car – which could travel at forty mph – from the Palace because it interfered with his lessons. While other boys could only dream of such things, Andrew experienced them.

He learnt to sail too, travelling to the Isle of Wight with nursery chum Kate Seymour and staying with her parents at Bembridge. He played on the sands with village children and learnt how to handle a small dinghy. It was an experience which paid off when he joined his father on board a friend's yacht, the sleek, green hulled *Yeoman XIX*, at Cowes when Philip took part in the race for the Britannia Cup. Although firmly strapped in, he proved himself an enthusiastic sailor.

How many children have gone to watch a soccer match with a Bishop? Andrew did when he was invited to watch Norwich play Chelsea by the Right Reverend Maurice Wood, the Bishop of Norwich, while he was staying at Sandringham. Norwich won one-nil although Andrew was equally keen to hear the news from his favourite club, Bolton Wanderers. He toured New Scotland Yard with an Iranian Prince, and on his eighth birthday was entertained by veteran clown Charlie Cairoli. His horizons were broadened when he visited Norway with his parents as the guest of King Olav. They sailed leisurely up the coast visiting the Prime Minister Per Borten in his farmhouse near Trondheim Fjord.

In spite of the VIP treatment he received, he was full of pranks like any schoolboy of that age. The chubby-faced youngster was the one who organised midnight feasts and mixed up everyone's shoes in the dorm. When a shirt appeared at the top of the school flagpole everyone's finger pointed at the less than angelic Andrew. He had a good tutor in practical joking in his elder brother Charles. It was he who changed round the signs at a Buckingham Palace garden party while Andrew kept watch. But it was Charles who had cause to complain when Andrew took his £4,000 Aston Martin for an illicit spin around the Balmoral estate. His love of pranks is a trait which runs through royalty. Composer A.C. Benson, who wrote Land of Hope and Glory, once commented acidly on royalty's: 'Odd fondness for ragging other people and laughing at their discomfiture when they are sure they will never be made to look foolish themselves.'

Joking aside, the fact that his life could never be completely normal was brought into sharp focus just before Andrew's eleventh birthday. The Special Branch had heard of a proposed IRA kidnap plot. Andrew or his cousin George, the Earl of St Andrews, were the possible victims. The plan was to hold them in exchange for the release of convicted terrorists. Gun-toting guards were drafted in and a round-the-clock watch was put on Andrew and his cousin. The Queen was informed and ordered that everything and everyone should behave as normal. In the end the plot did not materialise although the threat could not be ignored.

By the age of thirteen Andrew was developing into a rugged, self sufficent youngster, able to handle a gun, the wheel of a car or the tiller of a yacht. He was well fitted for his next school, Gordonstoun, a tough, uncompromising seat of learning in the north of Scotland.

When he was born his parents put him down for Eton but once his father set his cap at his old school, Eton was never really in the running. Philip, who left the school with happy memories was certain that Andrew would fit in. He commented: 'He'll settle down at any school once he finds out a smile and a bit of charm won't always get him what he wants.' Gordonstoun, near Inverness, was a curious choice to send Charles and Andrew and later Edward. It has no record of academic excellence and its sporting achievements are less than spectacular. Other Scottish public schools send their second and third XV's to play the school at rugby. What it does have is a reputation for toughness and spartan discipline. Early morning runs and ice cold showers were supposed to be the order of the day. When Andrew was once asked what he thought of the school he replied jokingly: 'The beds are hard and it's all straw mattresses, bread and water – just like prison.' The early morning runs were on the curriculum but by the time Andrew arrived they had degenerated into saunters and then only in decent weather. As for the showers they ran hot and cold.

The school indirectly owed its origins in the 1930s to German dictator Adolf Hitler. A German-Jewish educationalist called Dr Kurt Kahn had established a school at Salem in Germany based on the ideas of the philosopher Plato. He was imprisoned as an enemy of the State and it was only the timely intervention of his mentor Prince Max of Baden that saved him from the death camps. Wisely he fled to Scotland and established another centre based on the same principles in a handful of ruined buildings at Gordonstoun.

Philip, who had been sent to his German school as a thirteen-year-old youngster, arrived soon after when his own family realised that the Nazi regime could have dire consequences for the young Prince. In the early days everyone put their shoulder to the rebuilding of the school. Philip, together with the other thirty boys and masters, spent his weekends energetically mixing cement and laying bricks.

It was a fitting though bizarre apprenticeship for someone who would spend half his life with a silver trowel in his hand – although under rather more formal circumstances. Philip relished the life, was made head-boy or Guardian and had an outstanding record as a javelin and discus thrower.

By the time Andrew arrived, even though centrally heated rooms and carpeted floors replaced the bare boards and cold showers, many of the old ideals remained intact. The school's philosophy revolved around the idea that education should prepare one for life, not just university. Therefore the accent was very much on self-reliance and self-discipline. Even the punishment system reflects this. Discipline is based on trust. Instead of black marks, minutes are handed out to a culprit – two minutes for talking after lights out, three minutes for being late for assembly and ten minutes for smoking behind the cycle shed. At the end of the week the minutes are totted up and the culprit must spend these minutes on cross country walks thinking 'pure' thoughts rather than take part in the leisure activity they had arranged. The punishment is not supervised and the pupils are put on their honour to do them. Do they? Opinions vary. 'Of course,' says one old boy. 'You must be joking,' says another. 'If you had any sense you skived off.'

In the early days it was punishment enough for Charles just to be at the school. His belongings would mysteriously vanish to souvenir hunters and during his first few terms he made few friends and found the work difficult. But he got his head down and studied hard. He certainly made his mark, achieving the position of head boy like his father and playing the lead in the school production of Shakespeare's Macbeth.

Andrew however was in his element. The outdoor life appealed to his sense of adventure. Like his brother Charles he joined the school's coastguard service. Whenever the short, sharp blasts of the warning siren rang out telling everyone that a boat was in trouble he and his fellow coastguards would drop everything, even tumble out of bed at night, throw on their navy blue duffle coats and run at top speed to the coastguard station on the clifftop to keep a look out. And there was the added excitement of cliff rescue practice and lifeboat drill to keep interest running high.

Outgoing Andrew may have been too cocksure when he arrived. Wary fellow pupils called him 'boastful' and 'big headed' during his first days. One remarked: 'He had a bit of the "I am the Prince" about him when he arrived. He soon had it knocked out of him. The ribbings he got were unmerciful. He soon caught on.'

It was probably his desire to be one of the crowd that earned him the nickname The Sniggerer because of his seemingly endless supply of blue jokes. 'By the time he's finished a joke he's laughing so much you can't understand the punch-line,' complained one pupil. He quickly made friends with his easy charm and sharp sense of humour. In fact his high spirits led directly to him being rushed to hospital with a suspected fractured skull. He became involved in some dormitory frolics, bashed his head and in the morning complained to matron that he had a king-sized lump and headache to match. He was promptly driven to Grays Hospital in near-by Elgin for a precautionary X-ray. No damage was done.

It is interesting to note that while Prince Philip and the Queen favoured fairly conventional schools, Princess Margaret favoured a less traditional approach to education. Viscount Linley went to radical Bedales where the accent is on the arts, especially music and drama. Punk is fashionable and uniforms are definitely out.

At Gordonstoun, as at Heatherdown, there was nothing special laid on for Andrew. He had to muck in with the rest, making his own bed, tidying up the dorm and helping at school meal times. And the fact that his mother is one of the wealthiest women in the world didn't help – he only got £10 a term pocket money. 'He was never flush,' says one former pupil. 'He was always hard up like the rest of us.'

He showed a certain flair at woodwork, engineering and pottery. He even made two glazed vases as a birthday present for his grandmother. But it was the strenuous outdoor activities demanding quick reactions and physical dexterity which Andrew enjoyed most. He excelled at seamanship – a compulsory subject – and could raise a sail and pull an oar with the best of them.

He was chosen to crew the school's sixty-three foot yacht *Sea Spirit* on a sailing trip around the treacherous north coast of Scotland. After battling through a Force 8 gale he landed at Oban and went to a local hotel to 'tidy up.'

He was by his own admission sports mad, playing hockey, cricket, squash and rugby for the school team. Both brothers ended up with broken bones because of their intensely competitive natures. Charles came off from one rugby game nursing a broken nose, Andrew a few years later broke his foot. But it didn't stop him enjoying his brother's thirtieth birthday celebrations. He hobbled in to the ballroom doing a fair imitation of Charlie Chaplin with his walking stick and proceeded to waltz the night away as best he could. Andrew was also good at card games; all those hours playing with his mother had obviously paid off. School chums acknowledged that he was an excellent backgammon player.

During the school holidays he made a number of trips abroad, one to visit his German cousins, another to learn how to ski on the Swiss slopes. He also went with his mother on an official engagement to Dyce in Scotland. He stood beside her when she pressed the button which set the North Sea oil flowing into the brand new Grangemouth refinery. During his summer vacation he went round the oil rigs in the North Sea with his parents on board the royal yacht, *Britannia*.

He also undertook a three week visit to France with other classmates to brush up on his French. An elaborate subterfuge was laid on to put the royal bloodhounds off the scent. Andrew went as Andrew Edwards and even the teacher at his class in the Le Cousou Jesuit College in Toulouse didn't know he was coming until the day he arrived. Andrew developed the cloak and dagger element even further when locals asked him what his parents did. 'Oh,' he said airily, 'my father is a gentleman farmer and my mother . . . she does not work.' Have you ever tried to keep smiling through a 10,000 mile tour? She had every right to ask her scallywag of a son. His French improved considerably and his tutor summed him up thus: 'He is a lively boy with the good and bad points of any fourteen-year-old.'

His good points were definitely his keen sporting nature. And it led him to achieving a royal first that gave him more satisfaction than almost anything else while he was at Gordonstoun. He got his 'first' appropriately enough in the school's Air Training Corps. With the ATC he learned to glide – a feat neither Philip nor Charles had managed during their time at Gordonstoun. He went for lessons at Milltown, a nearby RAF base. Under the careful instruction of Flight Lieutenant Peter Bullivant he soon was in flight and Bullivant praised his 'enthusiastic' pupil. However, in order to qualify for his glider 'wings' he had to make a solo flight of the airfield. As he was not yet sixteen – the legal minimum for such an attempt – he had a frustrating wait. Just a couple of months after his sixteenth birthday he climbed nervously into his glider and made three four minute circuits of the airfield. When he landed he gave waiting photographers a cheery thumbs up sign. For once he had beaten his brother.

Although he achieved a royal first in the air, once on the ground he had to give way to his brother. When his mother came up specially to watch him in an end of term farce called Simple Spyman, Andrew was not in Charles' Macbeth class. He admitted: 'Charles is a better actor. Better at dramatics. I like to make a comedian of myself,' he added with a smile.

The young Prince was to enjoy himself thoroughly at his next port of call . . .

4 *Sweet Sixteen*

Sweet sixteen and never been noticed was the position facing Andrew when he joined his parents for the Montreal Olympics in 1976. His brother Charles was the royal heart-throb, Andrew was considered 'charming and polite' but not in the same league as teenage idol Mick Jagger or tennis star Bjorn Borg – in the pin up stakes. Under the watery Canadian sun he matured from a tousled haired schoolboy to a lean and fit young man with a gleaming grin and fashionably long hair. Canadian girls were not slow to spot the changes in Charles' younger brother. For once bachelor Charles was pushed into the shade as word went round that here was a new royal romeo. Later even Charles was forced to admit that Andrew was the 'one with the Robert Redford looks'.

But as Andrew made the seven hour flight to Montreal he had only one girl on his mind – big sister Anne who was competing in the three day event for Britain's Olympic team. He was keeping his fingers crossed that she would repeat the performance that won her the 1971 European Championship. He travelled to Bromont with the rest of the family to watch her ride alongside such household names as Lucinda Prior Palmer, Richard Meade, and Hugh Thomas. Her husband Captain Mark Phillips was also present as the team's reserve rider. Unfortunately for Anne there was no repeat of her European performance. Her horse Goodwill was restless during the dressage section, took a tumble in the cross country and ended up with time penalties in the show jumping. Anne finished a disconsolate twenty-fourth and was comforted by her husband and mother.

While the TV cameras focussed on Anne, the spectators had eyes only for one young man. Andrew was the hit of the Olympics. Everywhere he went grinning girls pushed and shoved to get a closer view of 'six foot of sex appeal' as Canadian newspapers described him.

Astonished aides had notes pushed into their hands by T-shirted fans asking for dates, leaving telephone numbers, party invitations, addresses and in one case a short poem. It was not the sort of attention he was used to as the girls at co-educational Gordonstoun had by now become used to seeing Andrew around. But his early blushes soon gave way to the Andrew style – a cheery wave and a few words of light-hearted banter.

The boy oozed confidence, a complete contrast to his elder brother who admitted that he didn't shake off his shyness with girls until he had left Trinity College, Cambridge. For Andrew there were no such inhibitions and, although startled by the attention at first, he soon seemed in his element.

In French speaking Canada the welcome for the other royals was not quite so effusive. The anti-monarchist majority kept a rein on their feelings but although the welcome was friendly it was very low key. The Olympic village was a different matter. Andrew flirted with a group of girl competitors during a tour of the village and was delighted when he was introduced to his new 'minder' – a bubbly blonde called Sandi Jones. She was the daughter of Colonel Campbell Jones who organised the Olympic yachting events. It was her job to show him round and keep him amused. The couple took an instant liking to each other and became inseparable. Andrew warmed to her sense of fun, she to his easy going manner. 'Call me Andrew, not Your Highness,' he told her as soon as they met. Sandi now says of their relationship: 'If we see each other over the years I am sure we will get together. We're very good friends. I am sure that in Andrew I have a friend for life.'

At the time commentators were vainly predicting wedding bells, citing the example of Silvia Sommerlath who had been a hostess at the 1972 Munich Olympics and ended up marrying Crown Prince Carl Gustaf of Sweden. Soon after, he became king and she was crowned Queen. At sixteen such talk was wishful thinking.

But this talk set a lot more young women looking at Andrew with fresh interest. He had already had one marriage proposal. When he was twelve, young Fiona Amey sent him a vain Leap Year proposal. But away from the glamour, Andrew's grammar was of more concern to his parents when they met Canadian Premier Pierre Trudeau. They consulted him over the possibility of Andrew studying in Canada for a couple of terms. The experiment had worked wonders with Charles when he went to Timbertop in the Australian Outback and Philip was enthusiastic about giving

Andrew a taste of another country. He even had the school in mind for he had been very impressed by the Outward Bound style of Lakefield College School near Toronto when he visited it during a tour on behalf of his Duke of Edinburgh award scheme. As an added bonus the school already had an exchange scheme operating with Gordonstoun and the 240 pupil school shared many of the principles of community service and self discipline which formed the bedrock of its Scottish counterpart.

To Andrew's delight there were rather more unusual and demanding sports on offer at Lakefield. He could choose between white water canoeing, rock climbing, langlaufing (cross-country skiing) or the rough and tumble of ice hockey. He immediately felt at home with his new comrades. He said later: 'The whole thing about Lakefield is the change. It is quite different from anything I have been used to. The school is quite excellent and so are all the facilities it offers. But it is not just that. The boys are terrific, really great. They are different from the chaps in England because they have a different outlook. Everyone in Canada is incredibly friendly. Life is very good indeed.'

One of the first people he bumped into after arriving in Canada under the assumed name of Mr Cambridge – one he was to use when he took Koo Stark on a Caribbean holiday – was old Gordonstoun chum Donald Grant, a doctor's son.

As he was being shown round the school he spotted Donald climbing a tree. He yelled out: 'Hey Donald, show us how you fall off and get back on again.' When he saw a kayak he asked mischievously: 'How do you drive these things?' Although it was fine for the boys to treat Andrew as an equal, the masters were under strict instructions to address the second-in-line to the throne as Prince Andrew.

No such formality hampered the dozens of young girls who lined the public viewing gallery at Toronto airport when he arrived. They screamed, blew kisses, waved their woolly scarves and in a refrain that Andrew would soon become familiar with, chanted: 'We want Andy' until he vanished into the airport Customs. But as his official car pulled out of the airport he wound down the window to chat to some of his puppy love fans. He talked about the weather and asked innocently if they 'did' Shakespeare in Canada. For his pains the teenager was accused of being 'boorish' and a 'snob' by a prominent Canadian columnist. At his first news conference he was relaxed and parried questions like a seasoned politician. He told a roomful of newsmen: 'This is the first time I've done this sort of thing. I'm only a nipper – not considered old enough for interviews with the Press.' He admitted he was something of a comedian; 'it seems to run in the family.' When it came to his pin up appeal he became very shy. 'No comment. That's too dangerous.' As for girls he admitted: 'I like them as much as the next chap.'

At Lakefield he had nothing but male company. But he wasn't complaining. Unlike his great-great-grandfather King Edward VII, who stayed at the college in the 1850s but with his own house and chef, Andrew ate with the boys, taking turns to clear up and act as waiter to other tables. His room at Wadsworth House, the former home of a pioneer family, was spartan, containing two bunk beds, a clothes cupboard and two chests of drawers.

His powerful physique and natural prowess soon saw him playing for the school's first XV rugby team. Rather than the tiny huddle of spectators who normally watch school games, a larger crowd gathered when Andrew took to the field. On the touchline local girls bearing sweat shirts with slogans like 'I'm an Andy Windsor Girl' and 'Andy for King' cheered his every move. Even the local Lakefield village joined in the general pride in having a royal son studying in the neighbourhood. The eccentric community, who had issued an order banning birds from singing at dawn, issued commemorative mugs and the local restaurant boasted 'Food Fit For a Prince.'

Andrew had a bash at ice hockey, scoring two goals but collecting an array of bruises that left him aching for days afterwards. Lakefield's head-boy David Miller said: 'He quite surprised me. He was quite vicious too and you need to be a bit vicious to be good at this game.' But Andrew was more modest. 'I wasn't much good really,' he confessed. However when he travelled with the hockey team to Pittsburg over the border he attracted a female following. But his charm was lost on one mother and daughter. When her daughter told her that a prince was in the crowd she asked hopefully: 'Is it an Arabian Prince?' 'Naw ma,' came the dismissive reply. 'Just the son of the Queen of England.'

Andrew tried sports that he would never have had a chance of had he stayed at Gordonstoun. In May he faced a late snowstorm during a canoe trip on the Petawa river and later he mastered the tricky art of windsurfing on a nearby lake. He gave his brother a few tips at Cowes but they both spent more time in the water than out, gleefully watched by Lady Diana and Edward who were sitting in a dinghy. Soon after he arrived he had the problem of finding a partner for the school dance. As far as Andrew was concerned the choice was obvious. It had to be Sandi Jones . . . but the problem was, how to invite her? To maintain maximum secrecy he asked a schoolchum to act as a go-between, but the plan backfired.

Sandi didn't believe the invitation was genuine and insisted on a formal invite from the headmaster's wife Sue Guest before she would come. Sandi said afterwards: 'I was flabbergasted when I received it. Although we took a shine to each other when we met at the Olympics, I had not expected to hear from Andrew so soon again.'

At the dance they shared non-alcoholic punch and doughnuts in between dances. Pony-tailed Sandi taught him how to do the Bump and his lessons took all evening. Sandi said afterwards: 'The ball was great and we danced cheek to cheek quite a bit. He learned the Bump pretty fast. Most of the time he wiggled and squirmed on the dance floor like any other teenager.' But the fact that Andrew only had eyes for Sandi did not go down well with the rest of the girls. Schoolgirl Patricia Foy complained: 'It was unfair that he had one girl all the time. A lot of us wanted to dance with him.'

But Sandi's time with Andy was not over. The next day they made their way to the ski slopes and for once Andrew left his Mountie 'minder' behind. He reached an agreement with him that he would keep in touch with a walkie-talkie if he would leave him free to be on his own with Sandi.

'Andy can be extremely resourceful,' said Sandi. 'He's just an ordinary guy who wants to have a fun time with his girlfriend.' As he waved her off from the platform at Coburg station he gave her a school scarf and badge and promised to see her again soon. He was as good as his word. They met later in Toronto, visiting a jazz concert given by Scots musician James Galloway. After the show they went for a quiet dinner at the Harbour Castle Hotel. Sandi's mother was quick to crush romance chatter. She described Andy as a 'charming young man' but added: 'Talk of true love is nonsense. They are only 16.'

During his stay he made plenty of friends and at vacation time he wasn't short of invitations.

Fellow Lakefield student Peter Lorriman invited Andrew to sample life as a farmer's son and join him on his father's farm in Orangeville in Ontario. He willingly accepted and helped tap the syrup from the farm's Maple trees. 'Quite delicious,' was his verdict. Peter's mother was equally impressed. 'Andrew is just like one of the family. It's been a pleasure having him here.'

Back at Lakefield he had another go at acting – this time playing the part of the elderly Mr Brownlow in a musical version of *Oliver*. But his performance hardly had the critics calling for more, especially when he vainly tried to revive poor Nancy lying dead in a gutter.

Sixteen-year-old Gillian Wilson who played the part was more than impressed. 'My heartbeat shot up to about 100 miles an hour when he put his fingers on my wrist,' said the star-struck schoolgirl. Gillian was not the only one impressed by Andrew. Teenager Linda Sergeant bumped into the young Prince while she was jogging through the college playing fields. 'He was really charming,' she said. 'I really fancied him.'

He flew home in time for his mother's Silver Jubilee celebrations – she had been on the throne for twenty-five years on February 6th, 1977. But he only played a walk-on role, accompanying his mother on a number of provincial visits. Tourists who went round a special exhibition of royal art at Windsor Castle were able to admire one of Andrew's paintings which reflected his Canadian visit. The view of trees, rocks and boulders was called 'Canadian Landscape.'

As part of the Jubilee celebrations he accompanied his mother on a short visit to Northern Ireland. The IRA had warned that there would be trouble. Sure enough the bomb threats came but the Queen went on regardless. Edward and Andrew travelled with her on board the royal yacht *Britannia* and the next day he sat behind his parents in an open Land Rover when they visited a youth festival. He listened to an all girl pop group before going on to a garden party. His stay in Britain was brief, travelling back to Canada this time in a more official capacity. He was soon in the arms of a pretty girl. At a party held for him at Government House, Ottowa he danced the night away with figure skating star Lynn Nightingale. He toured a number of wildlife parks as a member of the World Wildlife Fund, had a short but sweet reunion with Sandi Jones and then travelled on to Vancouver for the Canada Day celebrations.

When he visited the city he had a full programme of official engagements and his every step was dogged by smiling, cheering girls. Gaudily painted Algonquin Indians had a new name for him – Soya Hun or Heir of the Earth. He visited the local Pearson college and as he bounced on the beds he cheekily asked the college head John David what the sleeping arrangements were for the boys and girls. He went to a milling plant and then a helicopter whisked him upstream to a logging site where he stood in wonder as a 180 foot Douglas fir was felled. Then it was on to link up with brother Charles in Alberta to watch the famous Calgary stampede. Resplendent in a fringed cowboy jacket and matching hat he was a hit with the crowds – and hostess Gillie Newman who explained the intricacies of rodeo to him. 'A real Prince Charming,' she said. For the young Prince the most exciting part of the visit was yet to come.

He flew north to Yellowknife and then on to a small eskimo settlement on Ellesmere Island where he was shown how to make a kayak out of polar bear skins. But determined to land another royal 'first' he flew further north still, his plane landing on the ice at Cape Columbia, the furthermost tip of Canada's Northwest Territories. He had done it again. For no other member of the royal family had ever travelled so far north . . . latitude eighty-three degrees ten minutes to be precise. The Prince and his colleagues erected a cairn to celebrate the achievement, although it is probably the least visited royal monument in the world.

He journeyed back to Yellowknife where he met up with the Lakefield headmaster Terry Guest and a small party of boys. The plan was to canoe 280 miles down Coppermine river. It was a trip that went through sub arctic tundra, a wilderness land from which not everyone has returned. They slept in tents, living off dehydrated meat and beans and catching fish in the meandering river. It took ten days to finish the trip and Andrew ended up with callouses on his hands from paddling and his body badly bitten by the black flies which plagued them every day. In spite of the hardships he felt a real sense of achievement in completing a trip that few would dream about, let alone attempt. 'We capsized several times and the whole party ended up swimming,' he told fellow sixth formers when he arrived back at Gordonstoun. His two terms away had made a deep impression on Andrew as his schoolfriends were quick to notice. Schoolchum Georgina Houseman said: 'He came back more thoughtful, much more considerate and responsible.'

It was during his days in the sixth form that a cannabis smoking circle was discovered. Acting on information from Andrew's private detective, a number of students were questioned and several later expelled. There was some hostility to Andrew because his detective was 'snooping' but the vast majority accepted that Andrew had had nothing to do with the incident.

He passed his driving test after a twenty minute examination at Isleworth, Middlesex in a friend's car just a month before his eighteenth birthday. There was no big coming-of-age party for the Prince, simply a day spent skiing and snowballing around Gordonstoun. He was now £20,000 a year better off thanks to the allowance granted to him by Parliament. A spending spree was out for he was only allowed an 'appropriate' amount of £600 a year, the rest was put in trust.

He would have given all that cash to have attained the distinction his father and brother managed at Gordonstoun. For in spite of being made the head of Cummings house the glittering prize of head-boy or Guardian eluded him. Instead the Guardian that year was a girl, Georgina Houseman, a country vicar's daughter who was the first girl in the school's history to be made Guardian.

As a sportsman he was a real success, representing the school as cricket captain and in the school's hockey, rugby, squash and tennis teams. His headmaster Michael Mayor said: 'He's had to work jolly hard especially considering the distractions and commitments he has had.' According to some pupils the distractions were very much of his own making. Lucilla Houseman, the sister of the head-girl Georgina, was not so charitable about Andrew's talents.

Lulu as she was nicknamed told a woman's magazine: 'He didn't shine at anything. He loved having a good time. In fact the story going round the school was that he failed some "O" levels because he spent all his time reading trashy magazines and comics. He started school in the top stream but gradually went down except in French. He was very good at French. But he gave up Latin and went down a set for Maths. He was very very talkative. If there was laughter in the refectory Prince Andrew was bound to be at the centre of it.' The comments illustrate two aspects of Andrew's adolescence.

The natural teenage desire to be part of the crowd coupled with Andrew's aim to play down the royal role meant that he tried too hard to be 'one of the lads.' Even so his academic record was not as dismal as many people have assumed. He passed six 'O' levels, in English language, English literature, French, History, General Science and Maths and gained three 'A' levels after taking the exam under an assumed name in order to forestall accusations of bias.

The fact that he gained one more 'A' level than his elder brother was small consolation for not being made head-boy. And he was more than a little envious four years later when his younger brother Edward gained the coveted distinction. One visitor to Gordonstoun who was shown round the school by Andrew remarked: 'The one thing that seemed to concern him as he approached his final months at school was that he had not been made Guardian. He did not seem to worry too much at how he had fared at "O" level or what he was likely to achieve in his "A"s – although he was to fare quite creditably.'

But his growing attractiveness to women was also now apparent. One visitor noted: 'Andrew was already tall and well built – he certainly was very handsome. He appeared to be benefiting greatly from Gordonstoun's bracing and progressive atmosphere – though not entirely in the way his father had intended. There was one female for every two young males at the school although the evidence suggested that Andrew would have thrived even if the ratio had been less enticing.'

Along with his nickname Randy Andy came a new phrase, Andy's Harem, a joking but envious reference to the number of girls he took out. As Lulu Houseman revealed: 'He had several girlfriends at Gordonstoun as well as many friends who happened to be girls. His girlfriends were quite good for him because he took them fairly seriously and serious relationships are a steadying influence.'

First to fall under his spell on his return from Canada was Clio Nathaniels, the daughter of an architect who lived in the Bahamas. She was a striking 5 feet 10 inches brunette and along side the six foot Prince they made a well matched couple. He took her to the school dance and then to watch Charles play in the North Warwickshire Hunt's team event. She also met mother when he took her to Windsor for the weekend.

But Clio cause a stir when she unexpectedly left Gordonstoun and after spending a short time in London, flew home to her parents in Nassau. The gossip at the time was that she was heartbroken after her brief fling with Andrew had ended. But her mother, authoress Elizabeth Nathaniels, poured water on the theory stating: 'Andrew was very embarrassed about the whole affair. Clio was only one of his friends. She decided to leave the school after talking to me and her father.'

Undaunted, Prince Andrew took up with Clio's schoolchum, 18-year-old Kirsty Richmond. Their flirtation blossomed in the pottery class and she shared his love of skiing and tennis. They wrote to each other during the vacations and sent cards at Christmas and birthdays. He even gave her a huge box of hand-made chocolates as a festive gift. Sweet natured, well-mannered, witty and adaptable she was a hit with the Queen and was invited to Sandringham for Christmas two years running. When she went to church with the family she was officially listed as a guest of the Queen. But Buckingham Palace made clear that she was 'just a schoolfriend.' Even so it was a heady time for a teenage girl whose mother, a nurse, had scrimped and saved to send her to school. She was also loyal to the Palace code of keeping mum about the royals. She dodged every question thrown at her by eager reporters but her grannie, Annetta Taggart, did admit that Kirsty thought Andrew was 'very nice'.

'It was just Kirsty's turn,' joked other girls waspishly. Andrew was popular because 'he wasn't a bit wet, which is a nice change around here'. The choice of his first three real girlfriends is interesting. Sandi Jones, Clio Nathaniels and Kirsty Richmond couldn't by any stretch of the imagination be described as being part of the aristocracy. Though his upbringing was less formal than other royals he still tried to break free of too many royal fetters. To a large extent he opted out of the aristocratic dating game where mothers and matrons get together and plan romances with all the expertise of farmers discussing best beef cattle. But he hasn't kept entirely clear from the 'tiara mob' nor would he want to. He has attended many a society function and coming of age party of society debutantes. But the point is that he will ignore that world if he wants. As he once revealed: 'Because I haven't been the centre of attention, I've been able to lead my own life.'

To prove the point an American stunner called Sue Garnard was another Gordonstoun girl who caught his eye. Schoolchums said sagely: 'She is Andrew's long-term girlfriend. She doesn't mind

Andrew taking Kirsty home because she knows she is just a friend.' Like Kirsty, Andrew took her home to meet mother during the school vacation.

When he was in London he spent a lot of time with Julia Guinness, the younger sister of Sabrina, who was home from Paris where she was studying French. They spent their evenings at Annabel's, a plush, aristocratic nightspot, usually with a party of four or six. The discreet club is strictly members only. One night Andrew was barred from entering because he wasn't wearing a necktie. After a word with the doorman a tie was found and he was ushered in through the hallowed portals. Julia, who is now married to merchant banker Michael Samuel, says: 'He is a bit of a flirt but the most charming person you could hope to meet.'

When he goes out on the town he usually takes a number of friends with him. His normal tipple is Coca Cola but he has been known to sip a glass or two of champagne when the mood takes him. Besides Annabel's he can be seen at brasher places like Tramp or Tokyo Joe's in Piccadilly, dancing his heart out until the small hours. It was in his last couple of terms at Gordonstoun that he started to sample London's nightlife.

Newspapers began to carry pictures of the young Prince emerging from or entering some nightspot or other with a girl, usually a blonde, in tow – his detective walking a pace or two behind. Andrew's 'minder' is not to everyone's taste. 'He's a real passion killer, if you will pardon the phrase,' complained one partner. Rich, charming and good-looking, Andrew had all the qualifications to become a full time Hooray Henry. But as he realised only too well his future did not lie on the disco dance floor . . .

5 *High Flier*

What to do now? That was the problem facing the royal school-leaver and his mother, the Queen.

Go to university like his brother Charles? At the time there was talk of Andrew going to Clare's, the most intellectual of Cambridge's colleges. There was also the option of going into the family firm and spending a few years opening bazaars and touring factories.

Neither option appealed to the adventurous young man. He had his heart set on the navy and life as a helicopter pilot.

His success at gliding while at Gordonstoun had fired his enthusiasm and during his last school year brother Charles gave him a further taste of the high life.

Charles, who trained as both helicopter and jet fighter pilot had included in his tuition a parachute course and, in 1978 Charles had been appointed Colonel-in-Chief of the Parachute Regiment. Characteristically Charles was adamant that if he were to be inspecting the tough Paras then he himself must pass their exacting parachute course and win his own parachute badge.

To qualify, he took a refresher course at No 1 Parachute Training school and suggested Andrew joined him. His younger brother needed no second bidding, even if it did mean taking up two weeks of his school holidays. For Prince Andrew it meant starting from scratch. The groundwork was carried out with his feet firmly on the ground; how to fall and roll without breaking royal bones; safety checks; packing his own parachute.

Next step up from basic training was a jump from a moored balloon which passed without a hitch – which is more than could be said for Andrew's first parachute leap from an aircraft.

The plane chosen was one of the giant Hercules transport planes flying at 1,000 feet. The giant rear doors dropped slowly open revealing a patchwork of fields beneath the Prince's feet. His static line, which automatically pulls open the parachute, was clipped on and the Queen's second son stepped out into thin air.

Unfortunately, the lines of his parachute tangled and Andrew had fallen 200 feet before the Prince, cool-headedly putting into practice what he had been taught on the ground, spun himself around and twisted the lines clear.

Tangled lines are a common occurrence. It happened to Prince Charles on his first jump, who described it as a 'hairy experience.'

When Andrew was safely down on terra firma he confessed: 'Of course I was nervous. If you're not nervous you do something stupid. But I'm dead keen to do it again. Parachuting is an experience I would never want to miss.'

Andrew's second parachute jump was uneventful, despite the handicap of carrying a fifty-five pound oil drum in his rucksack as substitute for full kit, and the Prince proudly took home to his room in Gordonstoun the prized parachute badge.

That winter, Prince Andrew took the first steps to a flying career in the Royal Navy.

In December, 1978 he drove past the famous Hurricane and Spitfire proudly guarding the gates of the Battle of Britain fighter station at Biggin Hill for three days of intensive aptitude tests to see if he had what it takes to become a pilot.

Prince Andrew and eleven other young hopefuls had hours of written logic and quick-thinking tests, responses to lights and sounds to judge whether the royal reflexes were fast enough to cope with a career in the air. In one of the giant hangars, the young men were set puzzling physical tests; one test involved crossing a mythical stream with nothing more than a length of rope, some pieces of wood and several oil drums.

After tough interviews and medical exams at the Fleet Air Arm base at *HMS Daedalus*, near Portsmouth, Andrew had cleared the first hurdle to becoming a flier.

He had already gained his gliding 'wings' at Gordonstoun and during his Easter break in 1979 he managed to fit in a crash course at the RAF Benson headquarters of the Queen's Flight in Oxfordshire. Andrew was already showing an aptitude for flying and after ten forty-five minute lessons from a Royal Navy instructor, Andrew experienced the delight of his first powered solo flight in the humble little Chipmunk plane. His flying was carried out under the watchful eye of Lieutenant-Commander Sandy Sinclair, a former World War Two flying ace. His verdict on Andrew's ability in the air?

'He went solo much earlier than normal and appears to be well above average.'

Prince Andrew was in a somewhat more powerful aircraft, a VC 10, several months later when he accompanied his parents to the Commonwealth Heads of Government Conference in Lusaka. For the Queen, this exotic trip would hopefully sort out the thorny problems of Rhodesian independence and the formation of the newly-named Zimbabwe.

For Andrew, the trip was a welcome break between the end of his school career at Gordonstoun and the start of his naval career. It was the trip of a lifetime, touring national parks, and big game reserves, seeing Mount Kilimanjaro and Zanzibar.

And while his mother was engaged in heavy diplomatic chin-wags, Andrew and his father spent their time enjoying themselves.

On one sweltering hot day, father and son visited a farm close to Lusaka to visit people fighting to save the rhinoceros from extinction. Andrew, who had already inherited the family's keen sense of fun, laughed with everyone else when Prince Philip made a light-hearted jibe at the aphrodisiac qualities of the rhino horn.

The young Prince's inquisitive nature was already landing him in trouble during the tour. When he visited a Zambian copper mine an over-zealous security guard mistook him for a member of the Press when Andrew was separated from the royal party.

And in one village, when Andrew casually walked into a hut, flustered aides gently pulled him away explaining: 'No, no, this is for the goats.'

Everywhere the Prince went, he was

accompanied by a posse of press photographers eagerly recording his sunshine trip. In Botswana, a group of bare-breasted dancing girls performed a ritual dance for the royal party. The press photographers, their Nikons poised at the ready for a candid camera shot, watched the young Prince like a hawk. But Andrew, fully aware that he was the focus of attention, lowered his eyes and buried himself in conversation with officials.

The royal heart-throb was already a firm favourite of women from all corners of the globe. America's *People* magazine was to regularly list him in the world's top ten best-looking men. And Andrew look-alike Jose Conde earns big money posing for foreign magazines and newspapers.

His popularity was underlined when the American Bachelor Women's Society chose him together with tennis star John McEnroe, John Travolta, Warren Beatty and Woody Allen as one of the world's most eligible bachelors. President Rhonda Shear said: 'He's much better looking than Prince Charles.'

During the African tour, Andrew went walkabout in Dar-es-Salaam and a group of British-born wives waved a banner with the words: 'Hi Andy, come and have coffee.'

In Blantyre, one brave young woman went one further when the Prince walked into a restaurant where she was dining with her husband. The husband bet his wife £5 that she would not dare ask Andrew for a dance. She walked across to the Prince, and in her own words: 'The next thing I knew I was in his arms. Looking up into his eyes, such fabulous blue eyes.'

The African visit was wonderful, carefree fun

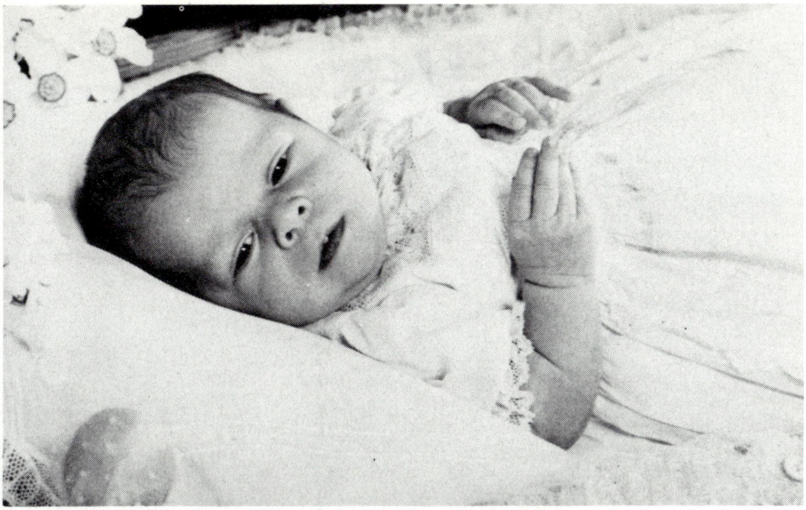

First official picture of the month old Prince. Taken at Buckingham Palace in March 1960 by Cecil Beaton.

Tongue-tied toddler Prince Andrew leaving Liverpool Street station after a five week holiday in Sandringham with mother. (Press Association)

After you. No, after you . . . Andrew and Viscount Linley discuss a delicate matter of etiquette. (Ian Elder)

Running wild . . . eight-year-old Prince Andrew and pals at play in a cub scout meeting held in the grounds of Buckingham Palace. (Photographic News Agency)

Bare chested Andrew paddling his canoe during his trip to Canada. Sergeant Pat Powers of the Mounties lends a hand. (Anwar Hussein)

Airborne . . . A delighted Andrew wins his gliding 'wings' at the end of his first solo flight at Gordonstoun. (Ministry of Defence)

Game for anything . . . Andrew finds himself on the losing side when Gordonstoun play Charterhouse at Oxford University. They go down fighting 3 – 2. (Bill Potter)

One two three, JUMP . . . Andrew and big brother Charles in a dummy parachute jump. And he's got his tongue out again. (Press Association)

Just like his father Prince Philip . . . Andrew on a pigeon shoot on a friend's private estate. (Daily Express)

Unaccustomed as I am . . . Andrew on his first public speaking engagement at the 100th anniversary of the Varsity rugby match at Twickenham. (Daily Express)

Watch the birdies . . . Andrew zooms into action during a run ashore at Port Stanley days after the Falklands victory. (Press Association)

Land ahoy ... Andy and flying colleagues aboard *HMS Invincible* hours before the joyful homecoming at Portsmouth after five months at sea. (Press Association)

Prepare for lift off . . . Andrew at Culdrose airbase before taking off for the fly-past during the Falklands tribute to British troops at Plymouth. (Press Association)

Salute to the Falklands fallen . . . Andrew after laying his wreath at the Remembrance Day Service at the Cenotaph. (Daily Express)

Andymania . . . A grinning Prince waves to the crowds after switching on the Regent Street Christmas lights. (Syndication International)

All in the family . . . Andrew and future sister-in-law Princess Diana leave Buckingham Palace in an open landau only weeks before the wedding of the year. (Syndication International)

Eyes down . . . Andrew keeps a low profile when he is caught in a Dartmoor pub with Navy Wren Kirsty Robertson. (Daily Express)

One of Andrew's old flames . . . former Miss UK Carolyn Seaward. (Daily Express)

Another of his old flames . . . model girl Kim Deas.
(Daily Express)

Hijack . . . the Prince makes a hasty exit from the holiday island of Mustique on a plane chartered by Daily Star reporter Andrew Morton. (Ken Lennox, Daily Star)

Andrew's first real love . . . soft porn film starlet Koo Stark, in a scene from the movie *Emily*. (Brent Walker)

in the sun for the playful Prince. But the following month, tragedy struck the royal family and the world.

Earl Mountbatten, a virtual grandfather to Andrew, was murdered by an IRA bomb on his boat while holidaying in the Irish Republic.

It was an outrage that shocked the nation. At the murdered Earl's funeral, Prince Charles wiped away a tear. It was a reminder of the dangers even Britain's best-loved family faced.

A steady stream of would-be royal sailors has flowed through the Britannia Royal Naval College, Dartmouth over the centuries. For some, rubbing shoulders with the citizens of Britain has not been a particularly pleasant experience.

Andrew's great-grandfather King George V had a tough time of it. Fist fights were the order of the day among certain cadets and many made a bee-line for their royal comrades. King George V said other cadets 'made a point of taking it out on my brother and I on the grounds that they would never be able to do it again. There was a lot of fighting among the cadets and the rule was that, if challenged, you had to accept.

'So they used to make me challenge the bigger boys. I was awfully small then and I'd get a hiding time and time again.'

Andrew's grandfather, the late King George VI, had it no easier during his Dartmouth days. The King – nicknamed Bertie – only got into the college by the skin of his teeth. The entrance exam was tough and in spite of extra maths and engineering coaching he only just managed to scrape in at the bottom of the list.

Once at Dartmouth, he was unmercilessly teased over his stick-out ears and stutter. They called him Bat Lugs and pricked his ears with pins to see if he bled blue blood. But he gradually settled in, despite one passage in his diary recalling the night he 'fell out of my hammock with the help of someone else and ended up with a black eye.'

Eventually, he was accepted by his fellow cadets and joined one gang in driving a flock of sheep into the local dance hall. On another occasion he threatened to paint a new statue of his father with red paint only hours before it was due to be proudly unveiled by local dignitaries. He was once given a whacking for letting off fireworks.

When Andrew's father Prince Philip arrived at Dartmouth in the late 1930s fist fights were a thing of the past but the navy's iron fist discipline was still very much in evidence; Prince Philip spent his eighteenth birthday digging a slit trench – punishment for one misdemeanour.

Prince Andrew arrived at the start of his twelve year short service commission on September 13th, 1979 and his first shave with discipline was the obligatory short back and sides. Training officer Lieutenant-Commander Jack Eglen said the prince muttered 'a few things I don't want to repeat' before marching off at the double for his appointment with college barber John Courage.

Andrew had arrived at Dartmouth in a brand new Escort RS 2000. Cars were forbidden to other new cadets for the first four weeks of training. 'They're too busy to touch one,' said Lieutenant Commander Eglen.

Also on his first day, Andrew lunched with the

head of the college, Captain Nicholas Hunt. 'Once this small official ceremony is over the Prince will be treated like any other midshipman,' said the college.

It illustrated once more the difficulties any member of the royal family faces when they try to break down the barriers and venture out into the real world.

Prince Andrew was following in the footsteps of elder brother Charles, a firm favourite during his Dartmouth days. When Andrew first arrived, he was resented by some fellow recruits. One midshipman, explained: 'He played the big "I am the Prince" routine all the time and seemed rather arrogant.'

The wife of one of the Dartmouth instructors added fuel to the fire. 'Prince Charles is still remembered with tremendous affection,' she said. 'But Andrew isn't popular with either the staff or his fellow cadets. His brother was a great practical joker. But Andrew walks away from anything like that. He never lets you forget who he is.'

To be fair, Prince Andrew had reason to shy away from too many high jinks because the following month Dartmouth and her cadets made headlines in every newspaper after a charity race ended in a major row.

The idea of the race was simple and proceeds were to be donated to the Royal National Lifeboat Institution. The race was between the Dartmouth college and their fierce rivals from the Manadon Royal Naval Engineering College in Plymouth. The Dartmouth task was to smuggle several firkins of beer through opposition lines to a tiny Dartmoor village called Milton Combe.

But the 'game' got out of hand with residents complaining of 'loutish behaviour' as the high spirited sailors manned illegal road blocks, frightened elderly residents and caused a minor road accident. West Devon councillor Lieutenant-Colonel Ian Greenlees wrote an official letter of complaint to the Ministry of Defence. 'Students behaved like drunken louts,' he complained. 'It was just a grown up version of cops and robbers with a total lack of responsibility. It made not one hoot of difference as far as I am concerned whether Prince Andrew took part or, not. I would say of all these men that they must learn to behave.'

Prince Andrew spent much of the 'game' trying to elude pressmen hoping for a royal snapshot. He roared out of the college gates in his black Escort and raced away with Fleet Street giving chase.

Prince Andrew said: 'I remember we were reversing up narrow lanes at forty mph and doing handbrake turns around corners trying to shake them off. It was great fun but they were very persistent.'

The persistence paid off when one photographer dived into a remote Cornish pub and snapped a shy-looking Andrew drinking with naval architecture student Kirsty Robertson. But the Prince had the last laugh when the pub landlord set his large dogs on the unwelcome visitor.

Whatever the feeling between the Prince and other cadets during the basic navy training by the end of the first of many navy courses, Andrew had earned the respect of officers and midshipmen alike.

The young Prince was fitter than he had ever been with an endless routine of running, hiking and swimming – always accompanied by long-suffering personal detective Inspector Steve Burgess.

The end of basic training is traditionally marked with a crazy passing-out parade where the cadets let their hair down and turn out in a mixture of odd-looking 'uniforms'. Andrew contented himself with a pair of pyjamas – a sensible decision because the order for the parade to fall out is rapidly followed by a jet of water fired on the midshipmen.

His first 'run ashore', as navy leave is known, attracted the usual crowds of pressmen at the Dartmouth gates at the end of the Prince's training. But, not for the first time, Andrew had the last laugh.

His name appeared on the list of cadets who were ordered to remain behind on duty inside the college. 'Pure Coincidence, simply the luck of the draw,' smiled a college spokesman.

The official passing-out parade for cadets at the end of basic training was an altogether grander affair for Andrew and the other £2,400 a year midshipmen. The Queen added a touch of glamour to the occasion and mother and son could not resist a swift smile as the Queen passed along the rows of uniforms inspecting the ranks.

Then it was time for a spot of leave. But for Prince Andrew, he's never really off duty. For, unlike his navy pals, the Queen's son must lead a dual life in the remote chance that one day he will become King of England.

The odds are firmly against Andrew – now third-in-line to the throne. But twice in the last century, the second son of the reigning monarch has become ruler, and Buckingham Palace never takes chances.

Since leaving school, Andrew has been 'educated' in the affairs of state and given a thorough grounding on how the country his mother rules is run.

When aged twenty, he saw what it felt like to sit in the Dock at the old Bailey while making a tour of the Building and sat in on the opening of a murder trial as part of his need to understand the workings of the judiciary. Later that year, he was guest of Prime Minister Mrs Thatcher at 10 Downing Street and listened intently to a series of top level briefings.

When he came of age at twenty-one, the Prince was made a Counsellor of State, replacing the Duke of Gloucester as the sixth counsellor. He can now deal with State papers in the Queen's absence.

If Andrew ever does become King he will at least be familiar with the nuts and bolts of the complex machinery that keep his kingdom ticking over.

His solo official royal engagements have been rare but there were never any doubts about Andrew's ability to carry on the family's famous tradition.

His debut public speaking engagement alone was as guest of honour at the centenary dinner following the 100th Varsity rugby match between Oxford and Cambridge. The bawdy post-match meal was not the easiest place to launch his lone royal career but Andrew scored a hit with the audience. In his ten minute speech he raised plenty of laughs – despite many drunken interruptions.

Back with the Navy, before starting flying training, Prince Andrew had to experience life on the ocean wave and in February 1980 he flew out to Florida for a three week tour of duty aboard the giant aircraft carrier *HMS Hermes*.

Andrew flew straight into the front pages once more after his first run ashore to a previously unknown bar named Trader Jon's Club Pigalle at Pensacola.

The club was situated in a sleazy area of the dockland and had the reputation in the area of being the naughtiest night-spot in town. It was famous for two things; a collection of military souvenirs – and an equally impressive collection of topless go-go girls.

Goggle-eyed Prince Andrew's picture of the Queen's son eyeing the leggy lovelies was wired around the world. Club owner Martin Weissman said: 'We were amazed when he came to see us, but he seemed to have a wonderful time looking at our pretty girls.'

His wife Elizabeth said: 'It was a real treat having the prince here. But Lord knows what his mother would have thought.'

The club had often been raided in the past by police after complaints by God-fearin' folk in Florida's Bible-belt but they stayed away that night.

And the Prince certainly had no complaints during his two hour visit. One of the topless lasses, Lindy Lynn said: 'He couldn't keep his eyes off. Now I know where he gets his Randy Andy nickname.' She later re-named her act the Randy Andy Eye Popper.

Another topless dancer, Sonia Larren said: 'He was a real Prince Charming. I didn't feel embarrassed at all. But I would imagine that the Queen would not be amused.'

The navy were unmoved by the publicity. 'When sailors go on the town it's only natural they want a bit of fun.'

Prince Andrew bowled the American women over. After the Trader Jon escapade the Queen's son was once more making news. The local US naval base launched a Dial-a-Sailor appeal to residents to help entertain the crew of *Hermes*. They need not have bothered. Once word got around that Andrew was aboard the phones never stopped ringing, with southern belles asking for 'that English Prince Andy, or whatever he's called.'

Prince Charles had also served aboard *Hermes* and the inevitable comparison between the two brothers began again. One senior crew member said: 'Andrew is very likeable but he's very conscious of being a royal. He's a bit of a mummy's boy. You could never say that about Charles. Charles would never need encouragement to join in the fun. And he certainly wouldn't talk about girl conquests.'

Whatever some crewmates thought, Andrew was determined to enjoy his trip States-side. On one day he slipped away for a visit to the fantasy paradise of Disneyland with the British consul in Atlanta, Mark Goodfellow as host. It was meant to be a private visit and the Prince even donned one of the staff blue coats to try and hide amongst the crowds. The disguise fooled some visitors – the Prince actually guided one innocent soul to an exit.

During his royal wander around the world's biggest fun palace Andrew shook hands with

Mickey Mouse and cartoon pals and found another pretty blonde on his arm. Cindy Greatwood, one of the prettiest Disneyland guides, was passenger with the Prince as they went for a 10mph spin in a toy racing car. 'It was magic,' said Andrew after the visit. Nobody enquired whether he was referring to Disneyland or the car-ride.

Pretty blondes and Florida sunshine were swiftly rubbed from his memory as soon as Andrew returned to the UK and the next stage of his navy training – the gruelling commando course at the Royal Marines camp at Lympstone. For ten days the Prince was put through one of the toughest physical training sessions in the world.

In full kit, he struggled along thirty mile route marches, he climbed and dragged himself around assault courses, and spent nights in the open on Dartmoor in sub-zero temperatures under freezing skies. And at the end of the course, the Prince came up trumps. 'We've put him through hell, and he's come up smiling,' said one tough commando officer.

It was a proud moment for Prince Andrew – odd one out at the passing-out parade dressed in navy blue amidst a sea of Khaki – when he was awarded the coveted Green Beret of the Royal Marines Commandoes. 'He is strong, physically fit but more important, he has determination,' said Lieutenant-General John Richards, Commandant-General of The Royal Marines, making the presentation.

The tough training was to prove invaluable several weeks later when Andrew began a course at Seafield Park, Portsmouth, designed to teach young recruits the art of survival in the rough.

The stiffest test the young sailors faced was a ten day stint in the New Forest armed with only a parachute for shelter. The idea behind the rough, tough test was to simulate being shot down behind enemy lines and force the young would-be fliers to think and fend for themselves.

Andrew was sent into the wilderness armed with the knowledge of how to kill a rabbit, skin and cook it. As normal, the Prince's detective went along – but the Prince's instructors insisted that the policeman rough it as well.

So for more than a week, the Queen's second son survived by setting traps for rabbits, eating wild berries, drinking from streams – and occasionally scavenging in litter bins for orange peel or left-over sandwiches discarded by day trippers.

It was a long way from the officers mess, and the splendid dining table at Buckingham Palace, but Andrew came through unscathed. A fellow mid-shipman said: 'Andrew was spared nothing. He had to do everything we did and he proved himself to be quite tough. It was as though he had something to prove – that he could do anything just as well as the next man.'

His next proving ground was RAF Leeming in Yorkshire where he was to spend twenty weeks undergoing elementary flying training. In practice, the Prince was becoming a fine young flier but his theory left a lot to be desired. He was christened Golden Eagle by mates – for his habit of dropping clangers in class.

Perhaps Prince Andrew had other things on his mind . . .

It was during his stint up north that the first of several much-publicised romances between the

Prince and a string of pretty girls began to fill Britain's newspapers.

They didn't come much more beautiful than blue-eyed blonde beauty queen Carolyn Seaward. Andrew and Carolyn, then Miss UK and runner-up in the Miss World contest, met in Devon. Carolyn, a statuesque 5 feet 9 inches tall with a curvy 35-24-35 shape, lives at Yelperton near the Dartmouth college.

The nineteen year old farmer's daughter hit the headlines when she told the world of her romantic candle-lit dinner with Andrew at Buckingham Palace. 'Prince Andrew is very charming, witty and amusing,' she said. 'After dinner we just relaxed, listened to music and chatted.'

Did the prince charming kiss her goodnight? 'That's one question I'm not answering. But I did tell my mum afterwards,' said the blonde beauty.

Buckingham Palace refused to shed any light on the cosy affair. A spokesman said haughtily: 'We are not prepared to confirm, deny or comment on such a story.'

Whatever the truth behind the romance, after Carolyn's 'kiss-and-tell' talks with the newspapers, there were no further sightings of the couple. Carolyn was later spotted at Wimbledon with fiery tennis ace Ilie Nastase after he announced the break-up of his marriage to wife Dominique.

But Prince Andrew has never been short of a pretty female companion. Since joining the navy he's developed a real sailor's eye for the opposite sex.

One pretty blonde, approached by Andrew at Cowes, explained the secret of the royal technique. 'He really laid on the chat for a good half an hour,' she said. Then he realised I was married and toned down the yo-ho-ho stuff. He certainly likes to flirt with the girls.

'He knows he's good looking but he's not conceited. He listens to what you have to say. He's interested in what you are and who you are. I suppose that's the secret of his chatting-up technique. He's genuinely interested in you as a person. He's a bit of the wholesome boy next door type. Really sweet but very fanciable. And lots of fun. He likes to laugh as much as anyone.'

After Carolyn, next pretty partner was model girl Gemma Curry who was with him at the Ritz for Princess Margaret's fiftieth birthday party. Gemma, twenty-two, met Andrew while her father, a wing-commander, was teaching the Prince to fly at RAF Leeming.

Despite his increasingly hectic romantic life, Prince Andrew still managed to get away from the girls once up in the air and flying. He left RAF Leeming and travelled the length of the country to the royal naval air station at Culdrose to begin the exacting task of learning to fly helicopters.

For eighteen weeks the Prince toiled away trying to master the rotary wings, beginning with the light Gazelle helicopter. So hard did the Prince work that he spent his twenty-first birthday in February 1981 airborne.

But all work and little play paid off. Andrew gained his 'wings' – and saved his father a day of embarrassment.

Prince Philip, like all members of the royal family, map their diaries out months in advance and his visit to Culdrose to attend the pilots' end-of-course ceremony was arranged long before anyone was sure Prince Andrew would qualify. For Prince Philip to arrive knowing his son had failed would have been uncomfortable for the proud father.

But he need not have worried. His son did him proud. Apart from gaining his wings, Andrew won the silver salver for the midshipman with the highest marks and was only a whisker away from missing out on the character and leadership trophy.

Prince Philip, dressed in his Admiral of Fleet uniform, made the presentations in April. He told his beaming son: 'Congratulations, good luck and happy landings.'

Then Philip, himself an accomplished aviator, told his son and the other thirteen successful pilots: 'This represents only the end of the beginning. There is a lot more training to be done and a lot more experience to be gained.'

For Prince Andrew, it was another royal milestone; he celebrated in style.

At a belated twenty-first birthday party at Windsor Castle he kept his word to Culdrose pals. He had promised them: 'It's going to be a hell of a party.' It was.

The 500 guests entered the historic castle under a spectacular canopy of laser beams. Once inside, another laser pulsated to the music. Rock superstar Elton John provided the cabaret; guest DJ Kenny Everett played everything from waltzes to punk for a sparkling guest list that included Prince Charles and his fiancée Lady Diana Spencer, Prince Edward, Prime Minister Mrs Thatcher, and several of Andrew's young ladies. Carolyn Seaward was present, along with the current royal favourite, twenty-two year old cover girl model Kim Deas.

Earlier that month, Kim – who met Andrew while he was dating her cousin Gemma Curry – had dined alone with the Prince at Windsor Castle.

But the relationship didn't last. Kim flew out to New York on a modelling assignment with friends saying she had jilted the Prince. But in the Big Apple she only had kind words to say about Andrew.

She said: 'I went to Buckingham Palace to see him and found him on his own watching television. He was happy that I was going to New York for the first time because it was something he couldn't do.

'He doesn't put on the Prince bit at all although I'm sure he wouldn't like me to say it. He's just a very nice young man under a lot of social pressure.'

As for those jibes about tagging him a male chauvinist pig after stories of Andrew getting Kim to help wash his car, the model girl said: 'He isn't at all. He's a lovely man, I don't want to say anything bad about him because he's still my friend. People think that because he's so good-looking he's not a nice person.

'But he's extremely sensitive and kind. He certainly doesn't live up to his nickname of Randy Andy at all. He's simply a good friend.'

So yet another beautiful girl walked out of his life. But as one left, another arrived – but this one belonged to big brother Charles.

It was The Wedding of the decade when Charles married Lady Di and Andrew carried the ring to the marriage ceremony televised around the world from St Paul's cathedral.

At the Buckingham Palace reception afterwards, clown prince Andrew was on his best form, teasing his new sister-in-law and telling the new Princess of Wales: 'You married my father.' During the nervous wedding ceremony Diana agreed to take the hand of Philip Charles Arthur George when she got her words twisted by mistake.

On the Palace balcony later, it was Andrew who was responsible for That Kiss. As bride and groom waved happily to the hundreds of thousands thronging outside the Palace, Andrew urged Charles: 'Give her a kiss.' Big brother obliged, to the delight of the nation.

And to see the newly-weds off in style, Andrew and Edward tied heart-shaped blue and silver balloons to the open landau taking Charles and Diana to Waterloo to catch the honeymoon train to Romsey. Completing the royal artwork, Prince Andrew borrowed a lipstick and daubed the words 'Just Married' to the rear of the horse-drawn carriage.

It was a busy family summer for the helicopter prince. Before the wedding, Andrew was godfather at the christening of Zara, second child of Princess Anne and Captain Mark Philips.

But by the autumn of 1981 Andrew was once more back behind the control of a navy helicopter, this time trying to master the large Sea King.

And in one exercise in the Firth of Clyde, the Prince gained first hand experience of practicing one of the Sea King and the navy's major tasks – air-sea rescue.

Andrew's helicopter was busily transferring

men from the Royal Fleet Auxiliary *Engadine* to the submarine *Ocelot* in howling wind and rain. Suddenly, seaman John Hendren was swept off the submarine's slippery deck and into the icy water off the Scottish coast.

Andrew, with his instructor seated alongside him, guided the Sea King down towards the waves above the head of the floating sailor. The winchman carried out the rescue, before the pilot prince took his helicopter and cold, wet cargo back to the safety of *Engadine*. 'He deserves a medal,' said grateful mother Mrs Shirley Hendren, of Wilfrod, Notts, who wrote to Buckingham Palace to personally thank Prince Andrew for saving her son's life.

Andrew continued his training success and soon qualified for his operational training certificate. On October 28th, sporting a 'full set' of beard and moustache, Prince Andrew joined the crack 820 front line helicopter squadron, at RNAS Culdrose.

When not on land, the Prince would be taking off from the heaving flight deck of the navy's newest carrier, *HMS Invincible*. His new role would be search-and-destroy missions protecting his ship from enemy submarines.

He was soon putting those skills to the test in a NATO exercise off the freezing coasts of Norway the following February.

One month later, a group of Argentinian scrapmen landed on a tiny island called South Georgia, 8,000 miles away on the other side of the world.

That insignificant action was to play a massive part in the Prince's future.

6 *Falklands War I: We are Sailing*

Twenty-year-old merchant seaman Michael Chapman thankfully clutched the grab-handle of the fluorescent orange life-raft tossed disdainfully about by the wicked South Atlantic waves.

Dazed, wet, frightened – but alive – the sailor had survived the bloody Exocet attack that moments earlier had claimed twelve British lives from the giant container ship *Atlantic Conveyor*. The youngster peered skyward with relief as the grey-blue underbelly of the Sea King helicopter hovered into view directly above his head.

'The weather was dreadful. It was very cold and the waves were about twenty feet high,' said Michael, from Retford, Notts.

Two dozen other dazed crewmates huddled in or around the raft. 'We were like sardines, one on top of another. There were four or five lads hanging on to the side of the raft because there was no room. They were suffering from hypothermia,' he said.

Some were burned, others injured. All were numbed by their terrifying ordeal of a few minutes earlier.

Chapman was one of the last to be winched up and away from the chill, wintry waters into the cramped, noisy confines of the Mark V Sea King, crammed with sophisticated anti-submarine sonar equipment. Aircrewman Tom Arnull swung him through the rear door, removed the winch harness, and guided him away from the opening.

Michael said: 'When I got inside the helicopter one of my pals pointed to the co-pilot and said "Look, it's Prince Andrew."

'At first I thought he was joking. But I looked up and sure enough, it was the prince. He was very cool, like all the helicopter crew. And he asked me how many more men were still in the liferaft. I told him there were a couple more and they were safely winched up. He and his crew did a great job.'

It was a meeting both the stunned survivor and pilot Prince are unlikely to forget.

Two young men, separated by the full width of the social spectrum, but thrown together by war. Fighting side by side; doing their duty as Britain battled to free the Falklands from the hands of Argentina.

They met in the midst of conflict, 8,000 miles from home, well aware of the risks and dangers they both faced. For war does not differentiate between Prince . . . or pauper.

And it was risk the Queen's second son was determined he would take.

From the moment a group of Argentinian scrapmen 'invaded' South Georgia, putting the Falklands and her islanders in grave peril, British Prime Minister Margaret Thatcher's mind was made up. Within days, Britain would assemble a massive Task Force which would sail south and grab back the islands if diplomacy failed.

Leading the way proudly out of Portsmouth harbour into the Solent would be Prince Andrew's ship *HMS Invincible*; and the royal sub-lieutenant was adamant; if *Invincible* went to war – so did he!

But first the twenty-two year old helicopter pilot had to convince Mrs Thatcher.

On Thursday, April 1st, Mrs Thatcher travelled to Windsor to see the Queen. The Argentinian Navy was heading fast towards the Falklands and the world was waiting to see how Britain would react. The Prime Minister told her monarch that invasion was imminent and said the government was adamant that Britain must defend her sovereign territory.

With the Queen in agreement, the two most powerful women in the land then turned to the more personal question of whether Prince Andrew – then second-in-line to the throne – should go to war.

Mrs Thatcher was only too well aware of the extra risks the Queen's son would face. He would be a prime target for attack, the one man every Argentinian soldier, sailor or airman would be gunning for.

Prince Andrew, at Windsor on leave from the naval air base at Culdrose in the far west of England, and his father Prince Philip joined in the discussion on his immediate future.

Andrew was adamant; he insisted on going to war. Indeed, according to some reports, the Prince even threatened to resign his commission if *Invincible* sailed without him. Prince Philip, a former naval commander himself who served with distinction in the Second World War, backed up his son's fighting stand. The Windsor family is not one for shirking responsibility, whatever the danger.

Mrs Thatcher left Windsor in no doubt. Andrew would sail with the Task Force, whatever her own personal doubts.

Soon after the night of decision, the Queen herself quashed rumours that her son would be spared from battle with a short statement from Buckingham Palace.

It read: 'Prince Andrew is a serving officer and there is no question in her mind that he should go.'

The following morning, April 2nd, Prince Andrew packed his bags, bid his parents a fond farewell and climbed behind the wheel of his blue 2.8 Ford Granada. With his personal armed detective beside him, they began the four hour journey west to Cornwall.

The Queen and her family, like every other mother with a serviceman answering the call to arms, hoped diplomacy would win the day and spare her son from battle. But it was forlorn hope. Even as Prince Andrew was driving to report for duty to Culdrose the invasion everybody dreaded was already under way.

Argentina's General Galtieri and his military junta announced that his troops had successfully attacked Port Stanley, the tiny Falklands capital. The tiny garrison of sixty-eight Royal Marines staged a brave gun battle but after several hours fierce fighting governor Rex Hunt ordered his men to surrender against overwhelming opposition.

By the time Andrew joined colleagues at Culdrose the Argentinian invasion was being debated in every home and every bar in Britain.

For most people, it was impossible to believe

Britain was going to war. Saturday, April 3rd dawned – and the Grand National was run as normal. Prince Charles and Princess Diana watched forty-eight-year-old veteran Dick Saunders win the nation's favourite steeplechase on Grittar and the Falklands were temporarily banished from many peoples' minds.

But the gravity of the situation was underlined when MPs packed the benches for a special Saturday sitting of Parliament.

And as the massive mobilisation of Her Majesty's forces moved into top gear at army barracks and navy ports, the Prime Minister revealed in public what she had discussed in private at Windsor two days earlier. She told a hushed House of Commons: 'The Task Force will leave on Monday – with *HMS Invincible* in the lead.'

The MPs were left in no doubt that Prince Andrew would be in the front line of any fighting.

But on the other side of the globe, fighting was the last thing on the minds of the Argentinian junta plotting in Buenos Aires. Galtieri knew his invasion of the Falklands had forced Britain into assembling a giant Task Force but he planned to halt the conflict long before any blood was spilled. He never wanted the mighty British armada to get anywhere near the South Atlantic.

His simple strategy was to pull Argentinian troops off the Falklands within a week and present it as a gesture of peace to the world. Then he planned to exploit it to the full at the United Nations and humiliate Britain.

Galtieri would have demonstrated that the Falklands were his to be taken at any time he desired – and the general could then force Britain into conceding sovereignty around the negotiating table.

Whatever the plans and counter-plans, Andrew and his colleagues from 820 Ringbolt squadron (motto; Shield and Avenge) were in high spirits as they prepared to sail in forty-eight hours time. But despite the tight schedule, Andrew still had time to fit in one more 'official' engagement before *Invincible* edged out of Portsmouth Harbour.

Sublieutenant Leslie Taylor, a close Navy chum since early training days and now a pilot in the Task Force flagship *HMS Hermes*, was getting married in Oxfordshire on the Sunday before the fleet up-anchored. Andrew was too busy to get to the church but he refused to miss the reception.

He managed to get permission for a last, brief spot of shore leave and raced to North Leigh to give bride Louise Woodford a congratulatory kiss. It was the last kiss the dashing young prince was to enjoy for many a month.

At mid-morning on the following day – April 5th – Andrew sailed off on the most momentous voyage of his young life.

The sailor Prince, standing to attention with shipmates ringing *Invincible*'s flight deck, had time to reflect what might lie ahead as tens of thousands of people watched the impressive flotilla glide away at high tide and sail to war.

Union Jacks fluttered, wives and mothers, fathers and sweethearts and children, shed tears, and cheered, as *Invincible* nosed out into the Solent at the head of the Task Force.

The Queen watched her son set sail on television at Windsor. It was the last time she would see her son for five anguish filled months.

Prince Andrew's thoughts of the future were rapidly halted once *Invincible* cleared the Isle of Wight. Her captain Jeremy 'JJ' Black headed for the open seas and ordered the flight deck into action. Sea Harriers screamed off the specially-installed ski ramp sticking up from *Invincible's* bow and Andrew, sitting in the right-hand co-pilots seat of his Sea King, lifted off from the rolling deck for the first of hundreds of missions.

Aboard the warship – ironically, at that time, due to be sold at a bargain price to Australia – nobody wanted to believe that this voyage would be any different from the NATO exercise off the Norwegian coast that *Invincible* had returned from several weeks earlier.

But Mrs Thatcher made it plain that if Britain had to strike back, strike back she would. In a television broadcast she told the nation: 'I'm not talking about failure.' Quoting Queen Victoria, she added: 'Failure? The possibilities do not exist.'

But in Buenos Aires the mood of Galtieri's junta was changing to one that was convinced that Britain would LOSE.

In the junta's war 'bunker' – the pink painted splendour of the Casa Rosada, the official residence where Eva Peron once plotted – General Galtieri and his Air Force commander, Brigadier Basilio Lami Dozo, were presented with a new strategy by naval chief, Admiral Jorge Anaya, the hawk in the three man junta.

The hard-eyed, unsmiling Anaya summed up his plan for success in two words: Prince Andrew.

Galtieri, customary glass of scotch whisky in his hand, listened in silence as the tall, thin-faced naval commander explained: 'This is an easy war to win. All we have to do is sink one ship – the *Invincible* – and Britain will crumble.

'For once the British learn that Prince Andrew's ship has been destroyed they won't have the stomach for any more fighting.'

Galtieri and Lami Dozo sat in stunned disbelief but Anaya dispelled any doubts by outlining plans for an audacious air raid in which the entire Argentinian air force would concentrate on Prince Andrew's ship.

So, unknown to the Queen and Mrs Thatcher, their worst fears about sending Prince Andrew to war had become a stark reality.

For, with hundreds of thousands of Argentinians joyfully celebrating the recapture of Las Malvinas in the Buenos Aires streets outside the junta's bunker, there was not a single voice that dare disagree with Admiral Anaya's plan.

Six ships of the Royal Navy have proudly borne the name *Invincible*. In the spring of 1982, as the newest of the warships steamed towards the South Atlantic, one odd twist of coincidence linked old and new.

The fifth *Invincible*, built on the Tyne in 1907, was a magnificent battle cruiser which saw action in the First World War. And after a bloody sea battle at Heligoland, she secretly steamed off at high speed to avenge a British defeat at Coronel – in the Battle of the Falkland Islands. She finally blew up at Jutland. All her crew, save six, perished.

Now, more than sixty years later, another *Invincible* was surging south to those tiny

Falkland Islands with revenge once more firmly in her gunsights.

The *Invincible* that Prince Andrew knows and admires was built five years ago and from her rakish stem to her workmanlike stern, the 677 feet long warship is crammed with the very latest technology. The 19,810 ton thorough-bred is the jewel in the navy's crown.

Her angled flight deck, 550 feet long, has the revolutionary seven degree 'ski-jump' to help pick her Sea Harriers from 801 squadron into the air more efficiently and economically. Up forrard, the empty launcher for the deadly Sea Dart surface-to-air missile stands manacingly awaiting its awesome cargo.

Her four Rolls Royce Olympus engines – the same power unit used on Concorde – sends a faint throb through the ship. At top speed, *Invincible* can cut through waves at an impressive twenty-eight knots and at her eighteen knot cruising speed she has a range of over 5,000 miles.

The 1,000-man crew are commanded by forty-nine-year-old Captain Black, a respected member of the Senior Service and a sea veteran on the oceans of the world.

The ageing warhorse *HMS Hermes*, twenty-nine years older than *Invincible* with rust streaks showing her age, was chosen as flagship of the British fleet by Task Force commander Admiral John 'Sandy' Woodward. But there is no resentment aboard *Invincible*. Captain Black had been given the vital task of air commander for the entire battle fleet. And he who commands the air commands the battle . . .

But in those early days, as Easter approached, thoughts aboard *Invincible* for Andrew and his crewmates were far from conflict.

The modern-day war ship was designed with creature comforts a main concern for the men at the Ministry of Defence drawing boards. The clean, crisp *Invincible* lines above deck are equally evident down below.

Like every officer aboard *Invincible*, Prince Andrew has his own private cabin. The cramped, eight foot by six foot room is spartan and a far cry from the luxury and lifestyle to which he has become accustomed since birth. The only furnishings are a bunk, a washbasin, chair and desk, but it's home.

It is also noisy. Living on 2 Deck, His Royal Highness sleeps directly below the spot where – two decks above – the noisy Sea Harriers land day and night.

In many ways, *Invincible*'s crew resemble a tightly-knit land-based community with the ship seemingly a small town. There is the obligatory ship's barber, and a significant Chinese civilian community providing a laundry – nestling directly beneath the Sea Darts – a cobbler, and a tailor.

They say an army marches on its stomach but aboard *Invincible* the Navy never seems to stop eating.

It suits Prince Andrew – a regular for cheeseburger and chips at London's popular Pizza on the Park – who, if he's hungry enough, can eat four times a day in the splendid officers' steward-service wardroom under framed colour portraits of his mum and dad.

If he drinks alcohol – which he rarely does – he can enjoy cut-price enjoyment at the wardroom bar where a healthy measure of gin and tonic only registers 14p on the mess bill.

But at sea, with flying a serious occupation, Prince Andrew stays strictly tee-total with Coca-Cola the strongest tipple to pass the royal lips.

And if the Prince ever begins to lose the battle of the bulge by over indulging, there is a constant round of physical jerks to keep in trim at sea. When the flight deck is not filled with planes and helicopters, super-fit physical training instructors put overweight matelots through their paces. Men can also play darts, table-football and table-tennis, or pick a book from the well-stocked library.

Video TV programmes are shown on TV sets in every mess scattered around *Invincible*. And the Prince and other officers can see an up-to-the-minute big screen movie three nights a week when the wardroom is hastily converted into ship's cinema. Andrew is normally first to grab a seat in the front row and usually recognised in the darkness by his loud guffaws during funnier moments.

The Prince becomes one of the lads the minute he walks up the gangplank and steps aboard 'mother' – the fond codename pilots call *Invincible*.

The only sign that he is someone special is the 'HRH Prince Andrew' name tag sewn onto the chest of his green one-piece flying suit. His pals in 820 squadron nickname him 'H' – for highness – and the Queen's son gets no special privileges.

Andrew's commanding officer, Lieutenant-Commander Ralph Wykes-Sneyd, explained: 'I think the Prince relishes his time at sea. It's probably the only place where he can be left alone. He gets no favours – and would be annoyed if he did. People can't believe that he's just another officer, but that's how we play it. The only people who find it unusual are strangers who come aboard.'

Once *Invincible* leaves harbour and heads seawards, Andrew can lead a life as near normal as he can ever hope for. His personal detective – constantly by Andrew's side – is left on the quayside; there are no photographers hiding around every corner awaiting an opportunity to snap the young prince; and no clamouring crowds jostling for a view of the Queen's son.

Andrew is a firm favourite in *Invincible*'s wardroom, buying his round of drinks and settling his monthly mess bill from his Sublieutenant's salary of £5,950.

When 820 – one of the more boisterous groups of navy fliers – let their hair down after a strenuous days' duties, the Prince is at the front of the squadron choir as the men crowd around the ship's piano and belt out some rousing version of bar-room classics.

Since the Prince first stepped aboard *Invincible*, he has made an effort to be welcomed by officers and men. He made an early guest appearance on the ship's own TV station and shortly after the ship sailed for the Falklands, plans were afoot for him to host his own show, provisionally titled: 'A dose of Andrews.'

Andrew occupied the guest spot in *Invincible*'s version of 'What's My Line?'! Lieutenant Nick

Bradshaw, then station controller, said: 'The Prince was a mystery guest and the crew phoned in asking questions to identify him. Nobody guessed - and when Andrew showed his face the ship was delighted.

'He's a great sport and a very interesting bloke. He realises the popularity of this type of programme and suggested the idea himself.'

Unfortunately, General Galtieri put paid to *Invincible*'s royal performance in the following months.

Andrew receives more than his fairshare of good natured ribbings from the wardroom but his 820 colleagues are delighted that they have a Prince amongst their ranks. And having a member of the royal family as friend and flying colleague has very definite advantages.

The last social get together for 820 squadron before they set off for the Falklands was a squadron dinner in the splendour of Buckingham Palace.

Prince Andrew had casually suggested the squadron had a meal at 'my place' and the helicopter crewmen, their wives and sweethearts enjoyed an evening they will never forget.

Escorted through the front gate of the house at the end of The Mall, past the famous guards, the squadron ate and drank the night away before posing for a memorable squadron photograph in the Queen's home.

A life on the ocean wave is nothing new for the young sons of Britain's monarchs. Andrew is simply following a long sea-going tradition that dates back to Queen Victoria's days. Her second son, the then Duke of Edinburgh, spent 35 years in the Royal Navy, joining up when he was only 14 and ending his career with the post of Commander in Chief, Plymouth.

Andrew's great-grandfather, King George V spent twenty years in the navy. He loved the sea and did not leave the Senior Service by choice. It was only the early death of his elder brother that forced him to take over as Prince of Wales and eventual king of the land.

King George VI, Andrew's grandfather, fought at the Battle of Jutland, and began his naval career at the age of thirteen. He was invalided out of the navy in 1917, much to his disappointment.

Andrew's great-grandfather on the other side of the family tree, Prince Louis of Battenberg, began almost as impressive a naval tradition.

The young Louis gave up his German nationality to join the great Royal Navy and fought to become First Sea Lord before losing the top-ranking post during the First World War because of his German background.

His two sons, George and Louis, both followed the naval tradition with Louis, later Lord Mountbatten of Burma, perhaps the most famous royal seafarer of them all.

He was captain of the famous destroyer *Kelly* during the Second World war, one of the top brains behind the D-Day landings, and when he became Allied Supreme Commander in South East Asia he ran the Japanese ragged.

Following his father's footsteps, Earl Mountbatten also became First Sea Lord and eventually Chairman of the Chiefs of Staffs Committee. His brutal murder at the hands of the IRA had a profound effect on young Prince Andrew, who had looked upon Earl Mountbatten as a virtual grandfather.

Prince Philip was also destined for a senior post in the higher reaches of the Senior Service until forced to quit, while captain of his own frigate *Magpie*, to act as consort with the Queen.

Andrew had a right royal pedigree to live up to. But in the first few days of the *Invincible*'s voyage south towards possible conflict he had no time to waste on reflecting on the past. Now, what lay ahead was his first concern.

As the giant British fleet gradually pieced together in the early part of the 8,000 mile voyage, Andrew and every man aboard *Invincible* began working up to tip-top operational performance.

The 801 Harrier squadron, under the colourful command of Lieutenant-Commander Nigel 'Sharky' Ward, had already put their awesome weapon power to the test. Two days out from Portsmouth, as dusk descended on the Task Force, Captain Black opened up the flight deck for *Invincible*'s crew to witness the destructive power of the Harrier's US built Sidewinder air-to-air missile.

One Harrier swept in low alongside the warship's port beam dropping a parachute target. Seconds later, another of the jump jets screamed in low and unleashed the Sidewinder. The missile, its tail glowing red in the blackening sky, surged through the air and blasted the target apart.

Prince Andrew stood with crewmates and watched, mesmerised, by the demonstration. As they trooped silently back inside from the chill sea air everyone was only too well aware that the next Harrier target might be an Argentine Mirage or Skyhawk.

The helicopter crews' role is less glamorous but no less important. Their task is to be the eyes and ears of the Task Force, constantly on the lookout for the enemy.

Day and night, in every weather, the Sea Kings fan out ahead and around the fleet trying to sniff out enemy ships and planes – but, most importantly, submaries.

Inside the Mark V Sea King, a complex mass of sonar equipment plumbs beneath the waves for the tell-tale ping of an underwater adversary.

Hour after hour, Prince Andrew and his colleagues roam around the oceans, skimming the waves at virtually zero feet, forever searching.

At set intervals, a sonar buoy is dropped from the Sea King belly into the water, hoping to find contact with an enemy submarine.

Prince Andrew is co-pilot of his Sea King. Senior pilot in the aircraft during the Falklands campaign was Sublieutenant Chris Heweth, navigator was Lieutenant Ian McAllister, and Leading Aircrewman Tom Arnull made up the four man team that was to mould into a super efficient war crew.

If the enemy submarine is detected the Sea King attacks with depth charges. On Good Friday, the fifth day of the voyage, Andrew's crew demonstrated the helicopter capabilities with a depth charge practice drop.

Minutes after his helicopter had lifted off *Invincible*'s deck, the ship's crew once more lined the ships deck for another fire power demonstration.

Andrew's helicopter approached 'mother' from astern. Wide on the port side, the Sea King suddenly dipped down towards the waves, dropped its cargo and soared rapidly skywards.

Seconds later, the ocean was torn apart as the depth charge exploded, shooting a huge spume of water into the air as the noise of the blast echoed across the water.

The Easter weekend for *Invincible* was light years away from life back home in Britain.

The first week at sea had been long and hard as the ship moved up a gear into a state of constant readiness. On Easter Sunday Captain Black gave his men the day off and it was all hands to the flight deck to grab a rare chance of sunbathing. *Invincible* was now slipping through the tropics and crisp white shorts and shirts replaced the heavy duty navy blue rig.

Prince Andrew stripped down to white shorts and sunglasses and soaked up the sun.

But nobody was able to relax fully. Easter Monday dawned and the Falklands blockade began officially with the introduction of the 200 mile Total Exclusion Zone.

Aboard *Invincible*, the talk once more turned to war and the ship's crew went through one of the many mock 'Action Station' alerts designed to close-up the ship, making her air and watertight within minutes of a real-life alert.

Once the dreaded klaxon wailed through the ship, every man donned comic-looking white anti-flash masks. Long white gloves, more at home on the arms of elegant ladies at the opera, complete the outfit. Funny they may look, but they prevent hideous burns.

Prince Andrew and the other airmen were each given a post where they must attend at times of attack. For sensible – but frightening – reasons, not all pilots are kept together. Andrew spent the alert at 820's briefing room or remained in his cabin. The realistic ship's damage control officer, Lieutenant-Commander Andy Holland explained: 'No ship can afford to lose all its fliers with one enemy direct hit.'

As the days wore on, the ship's company enthusiasm for mock alerts was bound to wear off but on Easter Monday, Captain Black instructed his munitions men to add a nasty note of realism to the practice.

Thunder-flashes exploded, reverberating around the sealed insides of the ship's hull, adding a necessary sense of urgency to the day's practice.

Day blends into day in a large warship at sea. This voyage was obviously different for even the most seasoned sailor in the Task Force – because none knew how long it was likely to last. Most exercises or voyages last little longer than two or three weeks and even on those short trips, it is rare for any navy ship to spend many days at sea without popping into a foreign port for an overnight stop.

Capt Black, and the skippers of dozens of other ships in the mighty armada, had to learn to pace the crew's build up to war. He compared it to running the marathon.

For Prince Andrew, the task was doubly different in one sense. Not only did he have to prepare to face the Argentinian enemy – his old adversaries were in his midst.

For the first time ever, a small group of national newspaper reporters were allowed aboard *Invincible* to cover the war. It was the first time ever that any member of the royal family had come under such close scrutiny.

It was a pressman's dream. We could live, eat and drink alongside possibly the most famous bachelor in the world. But when *Invincible* left Portsmouth the warning from the MoD representative coming along on the voyage was loud and clear; 'Prince Andrew is just another member of *Invincible*'s crew,' he smiled.

The problem for the pressmen was that Andrew was the only member of the ship's crew we were forbidden to approach.

For the first week of the voyage Prince and Press exchanged wary glances across the crowded wardroom, nodded briefly when we met unavoidably in corridors, and avoided one another at mealtimes. But sooner or later, something had to give.

Predictably, it was the Prince who made the first move. Despite reports to the contrary, Andrew is one member of the Royal Family who enjoys Fleet Street's insatiable appetite for anything and anyone remotely royal.

Andrew walked across the wardroom where we were gathered around the bar and bought a round of drinks. 'It's about time we introduced ourselves,' said the Prince, with a grin a mile wide. 'What are you having.'

From that moment on the Prince/Press problem evaporated. Indeed on some occasions it was difficult to get the Prince off the press's back as he wandered into a makeshift Press Office offering hints for stories to busy reporters.

Andrew was obviously totally at ease, safe in the knowledge that anything written about him would be censored before it was flashed back by satellite from *Invincible* to London. Every news story written aboard ship was censored not only by the MoD 'minder' but also by the captain before the ship's communications room was allowed to transmit the copy.

The Prince laughed and joked, dined and debated with reporters. Over dinner one night, he revealed to me his least loved Fleet Street adversaries. 'Charles and I have even compiled a hit list,' he joked.

He laughed aloud as he retold how he managed to give photographers the slip in frantic car chases as Fleet Street followed his racy black Escort RS 2000 around the lonely Cornish lanes near the Culdrose air station.

Now big brother Charles had been safely netted with a lovely wife, Andrew realised the spotlight would fall on him. And the two brothers had already compared notes on how best to keep love affairs off the front pages of Britain's newspapers.

In his time, Charles has used false names, addresses, false titles, even false noses, trying to give Fleet Street the slip. Andrew admitted: 'Charles has told me what to expect from you lot. I will be on my guard.'

Andrew shared his brother's sense of fun and is always game for a laugh. He positively enjoyed playing a harmless joke on one reporter as *Invin-*

cible sailed south. He confided the story of the warship's gyroscopically-stabilised pool table. 'It's remarkable,' he explained. 'However much *Invincible* heels, the table stays level and the balls don't roll around.'

After the hapless reporter disappeared, the Prince, helpless with laughter, told the rest of the pressmen: 'I hope his newspaper doesn't print that story. Any sailor reading that will know it's a spoof. It's the oldest joke in the navy. I should know, I fell for it hook, line and sinker, soon after I walked aboard.'

Andrew enjoys playing the court jester. But occasionally it can spill over into schoolboy silliness. Writer Roald Dahl's daughter Tessa once added an icy comment after a dinner party hosted by the enormously wealthy Duke and Duchess of Westminster. She said: 'At the end of the meal, Prince Andrew showed us what a sport he is by chucking endless bread rolls around the table.'

Andrew does enjoy seeing his name and picture in print but sometimes even he gets confused when Fleet Street links him with one more pretty girl.

He was an avid reader of the newspapers irregularly airlifted out to the Task Force – including the topless beauties in the Daily Star and Sun.

Several weeks before *Invincible* sailed, one particularly busty young lady called Joanne Latham claimed Andrew had entertained her to a romantic candlelit supper at Buckingham Palace. Her 'story' made headlines and Andrew was the butt of a succession of jokes in the ship's ward room at the time.

But the poor bemused Prince had never met the topless model. 'Who is this Latham girl,' he asked me one day. Luckily, Joanne's 34C body was draped across a Daily Star nearby and I showed the Queen's son.

After studying the busty beauty from every angle, the Prince said: 'No, I've never seen her before.' Then with a smile, he added: 'Mind you . . .'

Poor Joanne later admitted the candlelit supper never happened.

It was a voyage of discovery for the Prince and the Press, one possibly never to be repeated.

A discovery of another kind snapped the Task Force on full alert in the second week at sea when a Russian spy trawler, bristling with aerials, was spotted by one of 820's Sea Kings on a routine patrol. The trawler appeared to be in trouble and was being towed by a Russian merchantman and the Task Force swiftly left it in its wake.

But the following day, a Russian spy plane buzzed the fleet and four Sea Harriers were scrambled into the air to intercept. Shadowing Russian spy planes is something of a routine exercise for British air force and navy pilots in the North Sea but, spotting the Tupolev on the way to war sent a slight tremor through the Task Force.

But even as Britain teetered on the brink of battle, some naval traditions are never ignored.

The Crossing the Line ceremony is something every rookie seaman never forgets. For Prince Andrew, with the possibility of bloody conflict creeping closer by the hour, Friday, April 16th is a date forever fixed in his memory.

Invincible's rapidly suntanning crew were given most of the day off as the warship, gliding through the shimmering heat of the tropics, prepared to cross the Equator.

Every sailor crossing the line for the first time must go through a traditional ceremony before the mythical King Neptune that rapidly degenerates into a soaking wet slapstick show.

Prince Andrew – a gold coloured crown perched jauntily on his royal head and the words 'H–The Real Prince' stencilled on his waistcoat – tried to make a run for it when he was summoned before the 'throne' of King Neptune.

But five burly petty officers – King Neptune's 'bears' – were having none of it. To the delight of *Invincible*'s crew, Andrew was carried unceremoniously by hand and foot across the crowded flight deck and dumped in an undignified mess at the feet of the mythical master of the deep.

Andrew listened intently as his 'crime' was read aloud; positioning himself in front of television cameras so 'your mum will see you on television.'

The Prince pleaded not guilty but to no avail. Foul red, green and blue dye was daubed roughly about the royal features before Andrew was tossed backwards into a canvas pool of salty sea water. Once inside, his troubles were only just beginning. The five 'bears' grabbed the royal arms and legs and tossed the Queen's son high into the air – and back into the water, not once but three times.

One of the 'bears', *Invincible*'s wardroom chef Harry King, said: 'It's not every day you get to throw a member of the royal family about. If I did this in Civvy Street I'd be thrown in jail.'

But the Prince grinned and bared it as he dripped helplessly back to join his 820 colleagues locked in laughter at the royal dunking. The five pressmen, equally impressed and busily making notes for a story to send back to Britain, allowed Andrew to have the last laugh.

We too were given the Crossing the Line treatment, along with the MoD representative who was hiding on the ship's bridge high above the flight deck before several willing pairs of hands dragged him down to meet King Neptune.

It was a day of much-needed relief for Andrew and *Invincible* after nearly two weeks at sea with not a sight of dry land.

But the following day, Ascension Island suddenly loomed dead ahead on the horizon, her twin peaks a welcome sight.

For most servicemen with the Task Force, this tiny dot of land stuck in the middle of thousands of square miles of empty ocean, marked the point of no return.

Once past Ascension, nobody really believed the British fleet would halt until the Falklands had been liberated.

Diplomatic efforts were hastily continuing between Britain and Argentina but the Navy was taking no chances.

For two long days, the skies above Ascension were filled with the constant clatter of helicopters ferrying massive amounts of ammunition and supplies to warships massing at this midway point. The Sea Kings, with giant cargo nets slung beneath them, flew day and night. Prince Andrew was one of the few aboard *Invincible* to set foot on the island. 'What's it like?' said Andrew, taking a break between sorties, 'Red, dusty and very boring.'

Off-duty sailors spent their spare time trying to land one of the many sharks swimming sinisterly around *Invincible*'s stern - with little success.

The landfall did lift morale and the first, all-important mail from home swelled spirits even more. But poor Prince Andrew received no royal mail. While fellow officers clutched letters by the dozen, Andrew joked: 'I shall have to send a sharp message home about this.'

He need not have worried. The next batch of mail arrived within days, including a large batch for the Prince, including several from sister-in-law Princess Diana, who kept the Prince informed of the latest family news.

Sadly, Ascension Island disappeared almost as quickly as she arrived and with the move south, the mood of the Task Force grew sombre.

By this time, *Invincible*'s luxury and comfort had been stripped bare as the ship moved onto a war footing.

The colourful insignia on Prince Andrew's helicopter had been blacked out for security. Pictures and mirrors aboard *Invincible* were stowed out of harms way; anything that could move was tied down in case of attack and the dreaded effect of whiplash as the ship was hit. Even time spent undressed was kept to a bare minimum.

Invincible was now operating a twelve hours on/twelve hours off work routine for every crewman. Every sailor was ordered to sleep fully clothed and be ready for action at any hint of an emergency at day or night.

Several whales swam rapidly away from the Task Force with sore heads after sonar picked them up and wrongly identified them as possible submarine contacts.

Then came the first confrontation between Britain and Argentina. An enemy Boeing 707 spy plane was intercepted, then two more. Each time, Harriers screeched skyward to intercept but no shots were fired.

Invincible's crew received their war orders posted on the ship's noticeboard reminding all sailors of their duty to reveal only name, rank and serial number if the worst came to the worst and they fell into enemy hands.

Prince Andrew and other officers were handed personal supplies of morphine-filled hypodermic syringes with instructions to stab swiftly into the thigh to lessen pain if injured.

Andrew, like all airmen, was by now carrying a Browning automatic pistol and ammunition when he took off on a search and destroy mission for use if forced to bail out on land and sea.

Things were getting serious. Nobody needed to be reminded of the dangers that lay ahead.

But it was not only the Argentinians that the British fleet had to contend with. The voyage of liberation was taking them to some of the most inhospitable seas in the world. To make matters worse, the bitter South Atlantic winter was rapidly approaching.

Waves as high as tower blocks, freezing fog and howling gales are the evil trademarks for waters in this part of the world and it was the icy ocean that claimed the Task Force's first casualty.

A Sea King helicopter from the flagship *Hermes* ditched in freezing seas in the dark, black evening. *Invincible*, stationed several miles across the mountainous seas, was asked for assistance and Prince Andrew's crew were immediately despatched to search for the two man crew of the *Hermes* helicopter.

The South Atlantic was in full fury, tossing warships around like corks. Driving rain attacked the Sea King windscreen; occasional flashes of lightning lit up the scene in eerie silhouette as Andrew's helicopter edged forward a little above the waves searching for survivors.

After several minutes, their pale yellow searchlight caught a brief glimpse of an inflatable liferaft bucking wildly about below them.

Leading aircraftman Tom Arnull, on his first ever emergency, swung out from the tail of the helicopter and was winched down into the blackness as senior pilot Chris Heweth battled to keep his aircraft level.

Tom, twenty-four, said: 'There were flashes of lightning and sheets of rain as I was trailed thirty yards through the water towards the survivor. After three attempts he was just out of reach. But then he managed to grab my wrist and pull us together.'

Rescuer and rescued were winched back inside the comparative safety of the Sea King and the shocked survivor said his crewman was still inside the ditched helicopter. But despite further searches, only pieces of wreckage and the floatation bag from the Sea King undercarriage were spotted.

In the cold light of dawn, the dead crewman's

helmet was found, gently floating in the South Atlantic swell.

It was a tragedy every helicopter crewman flying with the Task Force knew might happen. Every crew had been flying long, tiring hours in the most atrocious conditions.

Prince Andrew, picking up the stunned survivor, learnt at firsthand, just how dangerous his war might be.

7 Falklands War II: Target Prince Andrew

Task Force commander Admiral Sandy Woodward, a keen fan of mathematical puzzles in his spare time, couldn't get his sums right as Britain and Argentina teetered on the very brink of war.

The red-headed commander was jubilant after the Royal Marines, in a daring dawn raid aided by inch-perfect naval gunfire, had swarmed ashore and captured icy South Georgia.

The Union Jack once more flew proudly over the snow covered rooftops of the tiny island capital Gritvyken and Woodward flashed a jubilant message back to Britain.

'Be pleased to inform Her Majesty that the White Ensign flies beside the Union Jack on South Georgia. God save the Queen,' he declared.

And twenty-four hours later, the scent of victory strong, the admiral warned: 'South Georgia was the appetiser. Now for the big punch,' even offering long odds against an Argentinian victory.

But the next day, in the cold chill South Atlantic dawn and after a gentle ticking-off from Whitehall, he had tempered his optimism with a degree of realism and told me: 'It could be a long and bloody campaign.'

The deadly game of brinkmanship between

Britain and Argentina finally came to an end on May Day, Saturday, May 1st, and Admiral Woodward – celebrating his fiftieth birthday – and his final sombre warning began to ring true.

The dramatic recapture of South Georgia was an important morale booster for the British fleet afloat off the Falklands but the final push was still to come.

And Britain's first, and most important task was to take on the Argentinian air force – and win.

First blow in the battle was struck shortly before dawn when two of the RAF's ageing Vulcan bombers blitzed Port Stanley airfield. It was a daring, long-distance raid with the giant V-bombers refuelling in mid-mission and, despite only scoring one direct hit on the runway, it brought the enemy air aces out fighting.

The war games were over and for Prince Andrew and every other soldier, sailor and airman, the days became terrifyingly serious.

For the first time ever, *Invincible*'s klaxon wailed out a genuine 'Action Stations' alert. The crew raced to their stations, hearts pounding, as ship's Commander Tony Provest warned over the tannoy: 'Hostile aircraft approaching from the south-west.'

Sea Harriers were already airborne and screamed off to intercept Argentinian Mirages closing in with the battle fleet firmly in their sights.

For Andrew and *Invincible*'s crew, wrapped in anti-flash gear deep inside the sealed hull of the warship, there was little to do but wait, and hope.

The Prince, reliving the horrifying first few seconds of a battle stations alert, said: 'To be told to lie down on deck of a ship is the most lonely feeling I know, waiting for either the bang . . . or the all-clear.'

For nine terrifying hours the Task Force defences held firm as wave after wave of enemy jets screamed in to attack, but the superb Sea Harriers were more than a match for the Argentinians and at the end of that first day three enemy Mirages and one Canberra bomber had been shot out of the skies.

As darkness cast a safety net over the Task Force, Andrew and his war-weary flying pals gathered in *Invincible*'s wardroom to hear the Harrier pilots retell the tales of their dogfights high in the sky in the biggest British air battle for decades. They had survived their first day of battle but many more lay ahead.

The following day, the Argentine air force stayed at home and licked its wounds. Prince Andrew lifted off into the freezing gloom for yet another search and rescue mission, skimming the waves for a sight or sound of the enemy.

But Andrew was relaxing off-duty when a young 820 colleague dashed into the wardroom that evening and announced: 'We've sunk the *Belgrano*.'

The Prince joined in the cheers as confirmation of the 'kill' arrived. The British nuclear submarine *HMS Conqueror* had intercepted the enemy's giant cruiser and sunk her with torpedoes. It was to be the first and last sea skirmish between the two navies but 300 Argentinians perished in the attack. And even in victory, *Invincible*'s crewmen spared a thought for fellow mariners lost in the freezing waters.

The war was going well for Britain. But on

Tuesday, May 4th Argentina delivered a crushing, devastating reply.

From the beginning of the voyage south, *Invincible*'s Captain Black had often mentioned what he considered one of the most dangerous threats to the Task Force – the Exocet.

The French-built fire-and-forget missile, slung underneath a Super Etendard fighter, skims across the waves at 700mph. Intelligence sources in South America had revealed that Argentina had limited supplies of the deadly weapon but on that fateful day General Galtieri decided to risk them – to horrific effect.

The jet fighter sneaked up to within thirty miles of the outer ring of the British fleet, hiding under the horizon before popping up and firing the Exocet.

The British destroyer *HMS Sheffield*, on picket duty protecting the two carriers *Invincible* and *Hermes*, had no chance of survival. The crew had just twenty seconds warning of the missile attack before the Exocet plunged into the heart of the ship, turning the vessel into a white hot hell within moments. Twenty British sailors died in the ensuing inferno.

Prince Andrew, airborne at the time of the attack, watched in horror as a thick black pall of smoke slowly rose from the burning *Sheffield*. He said: 'For the first ten minutes after *Sheffield* was hit, we really didn't know which way to turn or what to do. I was fairly frightened.'

The Task Force was locked in terror and confusion. *Invincible* weaved madly as the crew were warned; 'We are under missile attack.'

Across the ocean, another British frigate

unloaded depth charges after a reported submarine contact. A 'large underwater explosion' was reported but no wreckage appeared on the surface.

It was Britain's darkest hour. News of the tragedy sent a shock wave around the globe.

At dawn on the day after the disaster, Prince Andrew saw for himself the full horror of war.

The Prince flew over the still burning hulk of the once proud *Sheffield*. The black, charred and twisted wreckage would haunt him forever. On landing aboard *Invincible*, he said: 'It was a dreadful sight. It's something I never thought I would ever see – a British warship devastated.'

The Argentine junta was jubilant but Andrew and *Invincible* remained the enemy's target number one. Navy chief Admiral Jorge Anaya's audacious plot to sink the Prince's ship was still uppermost in Argentina's mind. A military spokesman in Buenos Aires chose the day after the attack on *HMS Sheffield* to remind the Queen and her fighting son: '*Invincible* is our priority target. It is a symbol, and if we destroy it, it will prove that Britain is not Invincible.'

Morale aboard *Invincible* was falling. It wasn't helped when the warship suffered her own first war casualties in a tragic accident that once again highlighted the perils all pilots faced flying in the wintry South Atlantic.

Harrier pilots John Eyton-Jones and Al Curtis had been scrambled to intercept a mystery radar contact that might have been an enemy aircraft. Taking off in thick, freezing fog, they raced to investigate and never returned. Radio contact was lost with the two jump-jets shortly after take-off and a mid-air collision is the likeliest cause of the two men's deaths.

A memorial service in *Invincible*'s huge hangar filled with Sea Harriers and Sea Kings was held several days later. Prince Andrew joined the rest of the ship's crew in a sad tribute to two popular men. It was yet another reminder – if one was still necessary – of the awfulness of war.

War veterans lightly dismiss battle as ninety per cent boredom and ten per cent sheer terror. That became the pattern for Prince Andrew and the Task Force for the next week. Naval frigates and destroyers made daily voyages close inshore to bombard enemy installations on the Falklands but the Argentinian air force, faced with thick cloud over the British fleet, were content to stay away and wait.

The emphasis was slowly switching from sea to land as Britain's crack undercover soldiers, the SAS and SBS, began making their feared presence felt on the islands.

Forty of those super-soldiers appeared on *Invincible* in the middle of May. Long-haired and often unshaven, they hardly resembled the disciplined modern-day soldier. But what they lacked in bull and square-bashing they made up for in bravery.

Several of the officers made friends with Prince Andrew over evening drinks in the wardroom. But it's doubtful whether even royalty was privy to their secret plans.

They were airlifted off *Invincible*, carrying massive backpacks and a lethal assortment of weapons, with no clue to their destination. But three days later their daring deeds were revealed to the world.

Forty five men of this undercover army had slipped ashore at Pebble Island under cover of darkness and intense naval gunfire and in the space of less than an hour had knocked out eleven enemy Pucara fighter bombers, ammunition and fuel supplies, and vital radar installations. British forces were jubilant at the success of the attack, carried out under the very noses of the enemy.

Prince Andrew and his colleagues began to make guesstimates on when the Marines and the Paratroopers of 3 Brigade, fast approaching the Falklands by sea, would go ashore.

By Tuesday, May 18th, the carrier group had rendezvoused with the troop-carrying fleet led by the assault ships *Fearless* and *Intrepid*, and including the requisitioned ocean liner *Canberra*. Prince Andrew spent his time in a ceaseless session of ferrying men and supplies from ship to ship as final preparations for the invasion began.

Back in Britain, Prime Minister Mrs Thatcher went to Windsor for her weekly audience with the Queen carrying a stark message. 'Diplomacy has run its course,' she said. 'It looks like war if we want the Falklands back.'

Peace talks at the United Nations, after weeks of fruitless debate, argument and counter-argument, finally ended in failure and it was time for the talking to stop.

After the evening meal aboard *Invincible* on Wednesday, May 19th Andrew and the ship's crew clustered around TV sets and heard Captain Black announce that British troops would go ashore on Friday.

Marines and Paratroopers would storm ashore at San Carlos and, as landing details were disclosed, Prince Andrew listened intently for he knew full well that this would be the day of reckoning for the navy and her fliers.

The Task Force would stand between the British soldiers landing back on the Falklands and no-one was in any doubt about how Argentina would react. 'They will throw everything they've got at us,' warned Captain Black.

Andrew and his 820 colleagues exchanged a few anxious glances for their job would be to protect the protectors. While Sea Harriers from the two carriers provided air cover for the troops, the Sea King squadrons would have to be at their most vigilant protecting the fleet from enemy submarines.

It would be an exacting day for *Invincible*'s crew but Captain Black, aware of the concern that might percolate through his crew, told them: 'I have every confidence in you. We'll walk it.'

The fateful Friday, May 21st, was Andrew's longest day of the war to date.

From dawn to dusk, as shipload after shipload of British troops scrambled ashore, the air above the Falklands was filled with battle.

Harriers pitted themselves against wave after wave of enemy Mirages and Skyhawks as General Lami Dozo's air force made a desperate attempt to halt the invasion before it started.

At the end of a bloody day's battle, in the air and on the Falklands, Britain had won the upperhand. The Union Jack once more flew over the islands and sixteen enemy aircraft had been shot out of the sky.

But the price was high. One Sea Harrier was downed, two Gazelle light helicopters were shot down by Argentine troops as they hastily retreated, and nineteen members of the SAS, a Marine corporal and an RAF Pilot died when a Sea King tragically crashed as it transferred the men from ship to shore.

Out at Sea, *HMS Ardent* was attacked by three Mirages that had managed to dodge the out-numbered Sea Harriers. Fifteen missiles smashed into the frigate and twenty-two sailors died as the ship's aluminium superstructure melted in the awful heat.

The following day, the enemy air force stayed at home but at dawn the next morning, the British fleet and land forces came under yet another massive Argentinian air attack.

With British troops already marching east towards Port Stanley, General Galtieri realised he had to strike early and successfully. But again, he paid a heavy price. Six more Mirages and two Skyhawks came down under a hail of Rapier missiles and small-arms fire as the enemy planes dived suicidally towards the San Carlos beachhead.

But another British ship was hit. A 500lb bomb hit *HMS Antelope*, anchored in San Carlos (now nicknamed Bomb Alley), but amazingly failed to explode. The ship was evacuated but during the night a brave bomb-disposal expert lost his life trying to defuse the bomb and *Antelope* sank, crippled by the blast.

By this stage, Argentina had lost fifty-five planes and British troops had gained a strong foothold on the Falklands.

Prince Andrew, exhausted after days of fly-eat-sleep-fly flopped into his bunk still wearing flying gear.

But like every British serviceman involved in the conflict, sleep did not come easily that night. Dawn heralded the 25th of May; just another date in British calendars but for Argentina, always a very special day, their national day.

And everybody realised this was day General Galtieri had to strike back.

May 25th was to live in Prince Andrew's memory forever. It was the date chosen by the three man junta to put into operation their audacious bid, discussed weeks ago, to knock out *Invincible* and Prince Andrew by Exocet and, according to Admiral Anaya, win the war.

The cost of mounting such an operation was bound to be high. Argentina's Boeing 707 spy planes had pinpointed *Invincible*'s position to 100 miles north east of the Falkland Sound, or about 500 miles from the nearest Argentinian air base on the mainland.

It meant a 1,000 miles round trip for the Super Etendard selected for the attack. The risks were enormous. Not only were they flying to the limit of their endurance, despite the ability to refuel in midair, but they had to face the Sea Harriers when they were furthest away from home. And the raid was made even longer because the attack was to come from east because Argentinian intelligence said the defences around *Hermes* and *Invincible* were spread to the west.

The enemy air attack began disastrously as *HMS Coventry* – on picket duty like her ill-fated sister *HMS Sheffield* – shot down five Argentine planes. But a second wave proved too much for *Coventry*. The ship was set ablaze when another group of enemy jets launched a bomb attack and seventeen crewmen perished.

Things were beginning to go as planned for the Galtieri junta. For the attacks on *Coventry* were no more than decoys for the real mission on May 25th – the attack on *Invincible* and the Queen's son.

Two Super Etendards, each escorted by four Skyhawks, sped low over the waves towards their royal target.

As soon as the aircraft radar locked on, two AM-39 Exocets were unleashed and the Etendards, their jobs apparently completed, turned and fled for home.

For some reason, the first Exocet sped harmlessly wide of the fleet still twenty miles from the point where the missiles were released.

But the second Exocet was heading straight for the heart of the carriers. *Invincible* and her defensive escort ships had little more than two minutes to take out the missile.

Radar-deflecting chaff – hundreds of tiny pieces of metal tinsel – were rapidly fired into the grey skies; frigates armed with Sea Wolf missiles swung swiftly into position between *Invincible* and the incoming missile.

Every conceivable defence system was thrown on red alert as the Exocet bore relentlessly down. But, unknown to Admiral Anaya, Prince Andrew was not aboard *Invincible* that day.

Andrew was hovering a few feet above the waves in his Sea King performing perhaps his most dangerous role of all – as Exocet decoy.

The theory is frighteningly simple. The Exocet locks onto its target from more than twenty miles away so the Sea King tries to place itself between ship and missile in a brave attempt to lure the Exocet off course.

Hovering twenty-seven feet above the waves – the Exocet's planned maximum height – the four man helicopter crew watch nervously for the Exocet and the instant it changes course and heads for them, the Sea King soars skywards and the Exocet passes harmlessly underneath before falling into the water.

Prince Andrew explained later: 'The helicopter hovers near the rear of the carrier, presenting a large radar target to attract the target. That's the theory. But on the day *Sheffield* sunk, one Exocet was seen to fly over the mast of the ship – and that's well over twenty-seven feet.'

While the Prince hovered dangerously above the waves, every Task Force ship in the vicinity armed with shells or Sea Dart and Sea Wolf missiles fired at the Exocet to try and knock it out of the air before it reached its target.

Today, with the war over, nobody knows exactly what system lured the Exocet off course but with just seconds to spare the missile veered off course.

But moments later, the giant *Atlantic Conveyor* was ripped apart by an Exocet. The 695 feet long container vessel had been hired by the government to ferry vital helicopters and supplies to the Task Force and was protected by the carrier group.

Tragically, twelve men died as the Exocet ripped into the *Conveyor*. No-one can be certain whether the missile aimed for *Invincible* hit the container ship but Junior Defence Minister Geoffrey Pattie, in one of the early reports on the Falklands War published several months later, said early indications showed that the *Atlantic Conveyor* may have been hit by a missile 'successfully decoyed away from another ship.'

For Prince Andrew, it was day to dread. Throughout the entire tragedy he was airborne but utterly helpless to prevent the dreadful loss of life.

He said afterwards: 'I was airborne when the *Atlantic Conveyor* was hit. We saw the odd 4.5 inch shell come pretty close to us and I saw *Invincible* fire her missiles.

'Normally, I would say it looked very spectacular but from where I was it was very frightening. I think the moment really sticks in my mind. It was horrific and terrible and something I will never forget. It was probably my most frightening moment of the war.'

But whatever his private thoughts, he still had a job to do and within minutes of the terrible attack, his Sea King was scouring the freezing seas for survivors from the stricken *Atlantic Conveyor*. Helicopter loads were ferried to warmth and safety and at the end of that dreadful day the Prince could only reflect on *Invincible*'s escape and hope that those who had lost their lives did not die in vain.

In Buenos Aires, the Argentinians were delightedly declaring the sinking of the Prince's ship. Newspapers and magazines were full of stories - not for the first time - of *Invincible*'s demise. One magazine headline proclaimed: 'El Aplastante Al *Invincible*' - A Crushing Attack on *Invincible*. Cleverly doctored photographs, purporting to show *Invincible* ablaze, added to the propaganda.

The propaganda-weary Ministry of Defence in London issued yet another denial over the 'sinking' of *Invincible* but it was another bad day for Britain.

The following day even the Queen could not hide her distress when she arrived in Northumbria to open the giant Kielder Dam.

At the lakeside the monarch, well aware of how close her warrior son was to death and destruction in the South Atlantic, glanced at Prince Philip and then told the crowds: 'Before I begin, I want to say one thing. Our thoughts today are with those in the South Atlantic, and our prayers are for their success and safe return to their homes and loved ones.'

It was a mother's concern shared by many and for the Queen, the agony lingered on.

By now, the battle for the Falklands was switching firmly to the land forces. The Argentinian air force was virtually beaten and the enemy navy and submarines had long ago apparently decided they wanted no part of the action.

The brave men from 2 Para scored a famous victory at Goose Green, despite losing their colonel 'H' Jones in a hail of machine gun fire, and the troops were yomping east across the islands in biting wind, rain and snow.

But twice in one week, the Queen was shaken with claims from Argentina that her son was wounded and in enemy hands, or that *Invincible* was once more a blazing hulk.

The Prince's sister, Princess Anne, joined in prayers for Andrew's safety when she made a rare visit to the local church near her Gloucestershire home at Gatcombe Park. She listened as a local policeman, leading the prayers, said: 'We continue to pray for all those involved in the Falklands, especially remembering Prince Andrew, and all who wait at home for news of relatives and friends.'

Twenty-four hours later, Britain suffered her bleakest moment of the war.

Fifty Welsh Guardsmen, other troops and crewmen died when the Argentinian air force launched one last attack on the British fleet. The Royal Fleet Auxiliary *Sir Galahad* was bombed as she lay at anchor near Bluff Cove. Sister ship *Sir Tristram* and *HMS Plymouth* were also hit, but fortunately suffered no serious casualities.

And it was on this black day that the Queen, unaware of the tragedy on the other side of the world, broke her traditional silence and attacked Argentina. She spoke out at a banquet at Windsor for her guests President Reagan and his wife Nancy. She said: 'The conflict was thrust upon us by naked aggression. We are proud of our fighting men. These past few weeks have been testing ones for this country. Once again, we have had to stand up for the cause of freedom.'

Those testing times were by now almost at an end. As Prince Andrew continued the cold, thankless task of patrolling the seas, British troops led by land forces commander General Jeremy Moore were marching triumphantly forward.

June 11th signalled the start of the last major offensive and, with continuous naval bombardment, soldiers stormed the peaks of Mount Harriet, Mount Longdon, Two Sisters, Mount William and Tumbledown as the beleaguered Argentinian soldiers began to wilt.

But there was still tragedy at sea, as a land-based Exocet hit *HMS Glamorgan* as she bombarded Port Stanley from close inshore and nine sailors died.

They were amongst the last casualties of the Falklands War for the following day, June 14th, Argentina finally surrendered.

White flags flew over Port Stanley, jubilant British troops marched into the Falklands capital after their meteoric 'yomp' across fifty miles of the most inhospitable terrain in the world, to be greeted by the delighted – and liberated – islanders.

One hundred miles away in the treacherous South Atlantic, news of the surrender was greeted with joy, then almost stunned silence.

Prince Andrew explained: 'When the end came there was no cheering and shouting, no celebrating.'

It took some time for the truth to dawn on the Prince and *Invincible*'s crew. They had survived the most dangerous days of their young lives. After weeks of awful conflict in which they saw friends and comrades killed, these youngsters had turned from raw rookies into battle-scarred war veterans.

Andrew said: 'We could not really believe that was the end of it. Everyone just looked at each other and said: ' "It's over then." '

But for the Prince, the Falklands War was far from over. Ashore, celebrations were quickly completed and the massive task of cleaning up the island began. At sea, the Task Force remained at its most vigilant.

Argentina had surrendered the Falklands and

General Galtieri had been kicked out of power as his price for the defeat. But the stubborn South American country refused to agree to an unconditional surrender. And back in Whitehall, senior military staff advising Mrs Thatcher were seriously concerned that one defiant member of the disgraced and discredited junta might launch one last desperate, face-saving attack.

For the Prince, tireless sessions of helicopter surveillance continued and with the Falklands winter rapidly descending on the British fleet, the dangers for every flier had hardly decreased.

Princess Anne, touring Denver, Colorado, summed up the dangers still facing her young brother when she told Americans: 'He is still flying missions in terrible weather. In many ways the weather is a more difficult enemy than Galtieri.'

But finally, four days after the Argentinian surrender, Prince Andrew and his helicopter crew got the chance to visit the island that they had risked their lives for.

On Friday, June 18th, his grey-blue Sea King touched down on the muddy playing field across the road from Port Stanley's tiny hospital with its giant red crosses emblazoned across its rooftops.

His first visit to the Falklands capital was supposed to be a private affair but the islanders quickly put paid to those plans, immediately recognising those famous features despite the anonymous camouflaged flying gear.

It was the first royal visit to the islands since 1957 when Andrew's father Prince Philip – himself then a serving naval officer – had stepped ashore.

Accompanied by his CO, Lieutenant-Commander

Ralph Wykes-Sneyd and 801 Harrier squadron's leader Lieutenant-Commander Nigel 'Sharky' Ward, a requisitioned Argentinian military jeep was put at the Prince's disposal and the VIPs were taken on a conducted tour of the island.

The battlefields around Stanley were still strewn with enemy mines and the few roads on the island were safe.

Everywhere the Prince travelled, he was confronted by line after line of dejected, defeated Argentinian toops, patiently waiting for ships to take them away from their private hell and home to loved ones. The young conscripts were a sad sight. They had fought a war many never wanted; land forces commander General Moore revealed hours after the surrender that Argentinian officers had actually shot bullets through the feet of some young conscripts in a grotesque attempt to keep them in their trenches as the British troops advanced.

At the blitzed and flattened Stanley airfield, Prince Andrew saw for himself the result of countless days continuous naval and Harrier bombardment. Crippled enemy jet fighters, their rockets scattered across the concrete, sprawled along the length of the windswept runway. Governor Hunt's official Cessna light aircraft sat crippled on the airport apron.

The Falkland Islands were in a desperate state, but they were once again British. And the islanders gleefully thanked their royal visitor for his part in their liberation.

Andrew, his cover well and truly blown, happily shook hands with delighted Falklanders, even posing for snapshots that would take pride of place in countless family albums.

What were his first impressions of Port Stanley after his 8,000 mile voyage? 'It's really a nice little town – a bit muddier than I expected. I am only sad that I had to visit it in these circumstances. But at least there is peace now and you can start thinking about the future.'

Then he quipped: 'It's a perfect place to bring my bride on honeymoon.'

Since the day many weeks ago that Andrew left Britain aboard *Invincible*, the sailor Prince, like every other member of the Task Force, had had no contact with his family back home. Letters were the only means of communications and during the height of the battles, even mail did not get through.

After the fall of Stanley, one of the first British ships to enter the capital's tiny harbour was the Royal Fleet Auxiliary *Sir Bedivere* – complete with her Marisat satellite-telephone communications system.

Every day, hour after hour, weary soldiers entering Port Stanley for a brief spell of Rest and Recreation, queued up outside *Sir Bedivere's* tiny radio room for a brief, emotional telephone chat with loved ones back home.

After his guided tour, Prince Andrew walked up *Bedivere's* gangplank, marched up to the bridge deck where the radio room was situated, and asked an astonished operator if he would ring the Queen at Buckingham Palace.

After the fifteen minute call, Andrew said: 'The line was so clear it was like speaking to London from Edinburgh. My mother was in – it was about the right time in the evening. She was quite surprised to hear from me.'

Amongst the Monarch's first words was praise for the men of Her Majesty's armed forces. The Prince said: 'She asked me to pass on how proud she was of everyone and to say how marvellously all the troops had done.'

After the long-distance telephone call home, the Prince revealed more details of his war but dismissed any claims of bravery.

'I didn't do a great deal,' he insisted. 'I have been at sea. But we did do quite a lot of flying in the last month and a half, when it really got intensive. We have done our little bit and the lads have done extremely well.'

The Prince did admit that one of his closest brushes with death came not from Argentinian – but British, missiles. Several times in the heat of battle, the automatic British Sea Wolf systems designed to pick off the enemy, mistakenly put the Prince's helicopter in their sights during Exocet attack.

Prince Andrew said: 'Sea Wolves locked onto our helicopter three times while we were hovering. It's not much fun having one of those fellows pick you out as a target. It really makes the hair stand up on the back of your neck.'

During the fighting the Prince's 820 squadron, already a super-efficient front line force, forged an even closer, personal bond. He said: 'My squadron has been absolutely fantastic. The spirit has been there all the time and I think the squadron really pulled everything out. I can only say it is a great squadron and I am glad I served with it.'

But the strain of the past weeks had left a mark of maturity in the youngster who went to war.

'I have been frightened,' said Andrew. 'It was

an experience but I would not say I would not have missed it.'

And, before strapping himself once more into the Sea King and flying back to his other 'mother', the Prince bravely admitted: 'If I had the choice, I would not want to go through it again.'

After the cheering visit to Stanley, Prince Andrew faced two more freezing months flying before *Invincible* finally headed home. The helicopter and Harrier patrols persisted and for *Invincible*'s crew, the enforced stay in the South Atlantic seemed never ending as other ships that sailed down with the carrier gradually disappeared and sailed home. *Invincible*, the first out, was going to be the last back . . .

But the endless days at sea were briefly forgotten on June 21st when news was flashed from Britain of Andrew's sister-in-law Princess Diana giving birth to bouncy Prince William.

'Congratulations on your demotion, "H",' shouted one officer as Andrew walked into the wardroom after news of the royal birth that shoved Andrew one down the line of succession to the throne.

The demotion didn't appear to worry the Prince, who broke his tee-total ruling and wet the baby's head in champagne.

A month later there was more cause for celebration for *Invincible*'s home-sick sailors when the government reversed its plans to sell the carrier to Australia. Armed Services minister Peter Blaker told the Commons that the government U-turn was a result 'of lessons learnt in the Falklands.' Australia, offered *Invincible* for a knock down £175 million, was offered *Hermes* instead.

By now, *Invincible* had been at sea for four long months and boredom set in. September had been pencilled in as the magic month when *Invincible* would be heading home but life aboard was becoming hard to endure.

Fortunately, the boredom factor had been recognised by the MoD and morale aboard the giant warship leapt with the arrival of an entertainment concert party – complete with three bikini-clad girls. The party was flown out from Stanley by helicopter and Prince Andrew, always one for an eye for the girls, enjoyed every minute.

The long-legged dancing girls, an act called Dream, had the women-starved shipmates delirious with delight.

Prince Andrew was captivated by one pretty dancer, curvy Carole St James, 28-year-old girlfriend of DJ David Hamilton, gazing into her eyes and singing a chorus of 'You made me love you.' And as the night wore on, the girls made a beeline for the VIP at the royal command performance. Carole and her equally attractive colleague Carol Hungerford were photographed sitting side by side with the Prince, a royal arm around each of them. Suddenly, some irreverent shipmate shouted: 'Andrew's pulling again,' as the Queen's son gave the girls a cuddle.

Carole St James said: 'He gave us a squeeze and a lovely cuddle' – and the pictures found their way on to the front pages of the British press. Even at sea, Randy Andy was making the headlines.

Finally, 145 days after leaving Portsmouth, the moment Andrew and his crewmates had dreamt of finally arrived and the ship prepared to head home. Her sister ship, *HMS Illustrious*, rushed through the builders yard, steamed past her older sister in salute to the Falklands veteran. Both crews lined the decks of the giant twin carriers as they surged through the grey South Atlantic with less than 200 feet between them.

It was an unforgettable moment. For half a minute the two carriers sped side by side. 'Good luck, keep it up,' was the message on a huge banner unfurled aboard *Invincible*. 'Well done lads, the *Illustrious* will remain Invincible,' read the banner reply from the brand new warship.

Finally, *Invincible*'s Captain Jeremy Black ordered a course north – and home to a heroes welcome.

Crowds had been arriving at Portsmouth since the early hours of the morning for perhaps the greatest welcome home for any ship of the Task Force. The Solent was alive with boats large and small, the air filled with helicopters and light aircraft all straining for a first glimpse of *Invincible*.

A light sea mist covered the sea warrior until mid-morning on that Friday, September 17th. Then the sun broke through and shone down on the Falklands star.

Aboard *Invincible*, many of the crew were nursing sore heads in the morning after the night before. Beer and spirits had flowed freely around the warship on the last night at sea at the end of a voyage of a lifetime.

In the officers wardroom, Prince Andrew had been in the front line of the 820 choir as they belted out songs until the small hours. But all hangovers swiftly disappeared as the royal barge, carrying the Queen, Prince Philip and Princess Anne manouvred through the busy Solent traffic and moored alongside *Invincible*.

It was an emotional moment for the young Prince as he was reunited with his parents and sister in the privacy of one of the warship's state cabins.

His family must have spotted a difference in the son they last saw five months ago. Andrew recognised a change in himself. Before stepping ashore to an ecstatic welcome from families and friends waiting on the quayside, the Prince explained.

He said: 'It will be very interesting going back to reality in the UK. It's been one hell of an experience.'

But then he revealed he was not altogether keen to be reverting from helicopter pilot back to Prince. 'I suppose I'm not looking forward to going back to being a prince. I would gladly keep going, particularly with this ship's company and with the men I served with down in the Falklands. I am obviously looking forward to going home but who knows what awaits me when I get home. I am sure I have changed somewhat since the Falklands.

'I guess I had to after seeing what I have seen and feeling what I have felt.

'I think my life has gone round the corner since I left Portsmouth in April. I have to pick up where I left off. It may not be easy. I have learnt things about myself that I never would have learnt anywhere else.'

In the darkest days, the Queen's son said he was determined to survive. 'During those moments when there was fear I overcame it with the simple maxim that I must think positive. I told myself "I am going to survive this."

'I was going to add "come hell or high water" but I won't.'

Whatever his feelings for the future, within hours of being back in sight of Britain, Prince Andrew's life had already changed. Two private detectives were amongst the first to come aboard while *Invincible* was still several miles out at sea. His valet was close behind ready to pick up the Prince's belongings.

Being home was to take a little while to sink in. Prince Andrew said: 'I daren't start thinking about plans for at least a week. I will wind down and acclimatise to life again in the UK, to the sweet smell of grass and the silence after the air conditioning in the ship and the noise of the Sea Harriers and Sea Kings.'

And what was he most looking forward to the moment he stepped back on British soil? 'A pint of milk – fresh milk,' admitted Andrew, fed on the powdered variety for five long, thirsty months at war.

But before milk came a jubilant welcome from the crowds on the quayside at Portsmouth. The Prince's parents walked sedately down *Invincible*'s gangplank to warm applause from the thousands decked out in Union Jacks.

Prince Andrew bounded down the gangplank and, once back on dear old Blighty, he leapt jubilantly in the air to wild cheers from the crowds. Someone handed him a single red rose which he clenched between his teeth with a wide grin. He was finally home.

It had been a voyage of self-discovery for the 22-year-old prince. He left Portsmouth an inexperienced helicopter pilot and junior officer. He basked in the affection the Queen and her family engenders across the length and breadth of the country; mums and daughters drool over the pin-up prince; the fellas cast an envious eye as the latest in a seemingly endless supply of pretty girls is pictured at Andrew's side.

In the early weeks of *Invincible*'s voyage to war, Prince Andrew appeared a curious mixture. At one moment young, almost childish; the next, a mature man of the world.

But afterwards, following weeks of endless flying, the Prince seemed to have matured into a battle-proven pilot who had stared death in the face and witnessed the full horrors of war. Some might say it was the making of the man. The nation must wait and see. But no-one can live through those dangers and not come out changed, older and, perhaps a little wiser.

8 *Koo and company*

After the excitement of the homecoming at Portsmouth it was time for Andrew to relax and spend a few days with his family. He travelled up to Balmoral for a reunion with his brother Charles and sister-in-law Princess Diana – and also to get to know his new nephew Prince William. As they sat around the fireside they listened with interest to his stories of life on board *Invincible* and his hair-raising exploits with his 820 helicopter squadron. No doubt brother Charles was just a tiny bit envious of the fact that Andrew had seen active service so soon in his navy career while Charles ended up as the commander of a rather unglamorous minesweeper. That Sunday his proud mother insisted that Andrew, dressed in a tartan kilt and jacket, sat with her in the car when they went to Crathie church, near Balmoral. During the service there was thanksgiving for the safe return of those who sailed – and a prayer for those who died in the conflict.

Throughout his time at sea Andrew had kept a secret that he refused a reveal even to his closest shipboard colleagues. It was his blossoming romance with American-born actress Koo Stark. They met that February at Tramp, the fashionable

London nightspot, which he often frequented. Andrew was on leave from *Invincible* and he and his friends were making rather a racket on the dance-floor. An angry Miss Stark stalked over and asked them to turn the volume down. But Andrew just grinned. He looked at the dark-haired young woman and her friend and said with a smile: 'Stop being so boring. We are having a great time, come and join us.' It was only then that she realised that she was telling off the third in line to the throne.

The couple chatted and danced, Andrew even splashed out on a bottle of champagne for the bubbly young lady who had gatecrashed into his life. It was the start of Andrew's first real love affair.

He asked to see her again and before he went to the Falklands they saw each other on several occasions. He visited her at her basement flat in London's Chester Square which she shared with her pal, Liz Salamon, a former gossip writer on a New York paper.

Then the Falklands war intervened. Before he kissed her goodbye he made her vow to keep their romance secret – not even to tell her parents. She was as good as her word. While Andrew was still at sea, Koo's father Wilbur flew over to London to stay with her. One night in August she revealed: 'Daddy, I'm going out with a really nice guy . . . he's very special to me.' But she never told him who he was.

While he was away Koo wrote and received a number of letters from Andrew. She airmailed a photograph of herself in a black T-shirt with the words 'Weird Fantasy' emblazoned on the front. She also sent two other photographs – one a full face portrait, another showing her in a skin tight costume. The pictures took pride of place in his locker as he sailed to war.

Koo was the latest in a long line of girls with Transatlantic connections. A line-up which started with Sandi Jones at the Montreal Olympics when he was sixteen. But Koo had by far the most colourful background. Koo, born Kathleen Norris Stark, is the daughter of Wilbur Stark, a successful Hollywood film producer. Her mother is the former actress Kathy Norris. She was sent to Miss Hewitt's Private School for Young Ladies in New York but by then her parents had divorced. Her mother is now happily married for the third time to Carl Caruso, a retired TV announcer. She moved to England in 1975. The striking, dark-haired young girl had one ambition in life – to be a successful film actress. But she found early on that the road to success is paved not with gold but blue – blue firms to be precise. The only parts the young hopeful was offered were in soft porn movies. Her first break came in 1977 when she starred in *Emily*, made by the Earl of Pembroke.

The film, which has gained new notoriety because of Koo's involvement, featured her in a lesbian shower scene with actress Ina Skriver. Later Koo talked without embarrassment about her feelings and how she coped with explicit scenes – including a masturbation sequence. 'I felt very vulnerable. That masturbation scene was difficult because in my personal experience it has never done anything for me. Emily was supposed to be seventeen, had not made love to any man before and what she was doing was just giving herself innocent pleasure. It was not the sort of masturbation where she was imagining a man making love.'

About that now infamous lesbian shower scene she says: 'We were not given any direction at all. But by the time we came to shoot, it was running very late and people were arriving on the set at Shepperton for the end of picture party. I looked around and suddenly thought: "Hell, I'm naked and in front of all these people too." I got them cleared off immediately. These people were staring and making me feel terrible. By this time tension was really high. Ina got into the shower and gave me a really hard back massage. When I was kissing her body I had to close my eyes because of the water and I could only tell where I was by touching her breast or around her waist. It was only afterwards that the strain hit me mentally. I felt so drained I could hardly stand.'

Whatever the mechanics of filming, the role earned her the title of the British answer to Emmanuelle. It was a title she was later to regret. But her porn acting career didn't stop there. She starred in *Cruel Passions*, a work based on the life of the Marquis de Sade. She played Justine, a young girl who refuses to pleasure some nuns, is sodomised by Lord Carlisle, savaged by dogs and raped by two grave robbers. Finally her body is thrown into a lake. Hardly the stuff Oscar winning performances are made of.

She made her TV debut in a play called *The Blue Film* which had to be put on late at night because Koo featured in explicit sex scenes. She remembers that play with some embarrassment. 'I was with an actor who had what I would call a physical reaction to my body,' she says. 'He and I were chatting for about fifteen minutes lying a couple of feet apart in the bed waiting for all the lighting men to get things together to shoot the scene. As soon as our bodies touched I thought: "Oh dear" and got out of the bed right away. The director gave him a couple of minutes to cool off. He was very embarrassed.'

Understandably Koo has many regrets about her porn past. She said afterwards: 'I never wanted to do an erotic film but that's about all that's being produced.' And she was not keen on the atmosphere surrounding the making of such films. 'I hate jokes about nudity on set. Some technicians try it on and make cracks, attempting to be ultra casual. That I can't stand nor that sort of man either. In fact I hate men who are crude about sex. It is a subject which should be treated with sensitivity and love.'

She is less confident about her own sex appeal away from the camera lights. 'I feel very insecure at times. I hate my bottom. It looks so fat and I have a thing about it.' In a bid to escape the blue side of the film world she flew to New York when she was twenty-one to go for a course of acting lessons. On her return to London she met and fell and in love with millionaire Robert Winsor, the ex-husband of her actress friend Valli Kemp, the former Miss Australia and Miss World contestant. She lived with him in his North London home but the day before the couple were due to wed she got cold feet and called the whole thing off. Although her love life was suffering her acting career was now on the move. She landed a number of small parts in TV plays and in films like *Star Wars* and *The Rocky Horror Show*. And to try her hand at more serious drama she went to the National Theatre where she understudied in *Who's Afraid of Virginia Woolf?* This was the exotic background of the girl Prince Andrew was now dating, a girl whose father once gave her this advice: 'If you can't eat out at the best place in town, stay at home and eat a banana.' Although polite society was taken aback when the film career of Andrew's girlfriend was laid bare, he could comfort himself with the thought that he was merely carrying on a grand old royal tradition. The princely dalliance with actresses goes right back to the days of Nell Gwynn and her riotous affair with Charles II. Charles thought so highly of her that even on his deathbed he was heard to gasp: 'Let not poor Nelly starve.' She managed to scrape by although his death did scupper her chances of becoming the Duchess of Greenwich. Nell wasn't Charles' only actress lover. Moll Davies and Lucy Walters were two other dramatis personae in the King's bedchamber. George I celebrated the death of his wife by going to the theatre and flirting with the assembled actresses.

Even under the rigid reign of Queen Victoria the royal romance with the stage continued. When the Prince of Wales – later Edward VII – was sent on a ten week army course to Ireland he was still a virgin. But his fellow Guards officers decided to end that state of affairs. They smuggled into their Curagh barracks a music hall singer and bit part actress called Nellie Clifden. She was the friend of Lord Carrington, a fellow officer who was prepared to sacrifice his lady to royalty. He later became

Governor of New South Wales.

Lord Suffield made a similar sacrifice with actress Lily Langtry who made her debut at the Haymarket in 1881. After their introduction Edward and Lily remained constant companions. And the tradition has continued to the present day. Prince Charles had a brief fling with actress Susan George who was later offered £100,000 to spill the beans on her royal romance. She refused.

And so to Koo, the latest in an honourable tradition. She saw in Andrew many of the qualities she wanted in a man.

Her ideal is dark haired, six foot tall, self assured and with narrow hips. It was a description she gave when she made a TV documentary called Quest For Love in which she also talked frankly about her career in porn films. She gave her description before she met Andrew but with hindsight it sounds uncannily like the young Prince.

'I particularly like strong hands,' she said. 'They should be delicate yet strong. A man with sensitive hands is often sensitive about other things as well.' She also thought that a man should be knowledgable about films and art 'so that he can appreciate what I do for a living and my need to do it.'

Whether Andrew knew the full details about her career while he was taking her out only he can say. But one thing is certain. Andrew is a strong willed young man, like the rest of his family. If he had set his cap at a girl he would stand by her, no matter what. Indeed the fact that he is still seeing her long after the hulabaloo has died down proves the point.

At first their romance was kept secret. No-one knew that the couple were writing to each other while Andrew spent long, lonely hours on board *Invincible*. The mail drops were the highlight of life at sea and the further south the Task Force went the more a letter from home was treasured. But Koo wasn't the only girl he wrote to. He sent a 'long, long' letter to former girlfriend Carolyn Seaward and kept up with all the latest family gossip from Princess Diana.

He told shipmates that there were four women in his life – his grandmother, his mother, sister Anne and sister-in-law Diana. He added with a smile that there was one woman outside the royal circle although wild horses wouldn't drag the identity of the mystery woman out of him. As soon as he returned he was on the phone to the 'mystery woman' and asked Koo to Balmoral to meet the rest of the family. By all accounts the Queen was very impressed.

She took an immediate liking to the bubbly, high-spirited young woman who had made such a lasting impression on her son. And Koo caused a few raised eyebrows among the male members of the family when she arrived for dinner one evening dressed in the briefest of gold ra-ra skirts. Andrew no doubt gave her a cheeky wink when she walked in.

It was while he was at Balmoral that his aunt, Princess Margaret, offered him the use of her holiday home, Jolies Eaux, on the romantic Caribbean island of Mustique. It was an offer he was delighted to accept – a just reward for all those days on the High Seas. Koo of course was invited as well.

Days before they left for their Caribbean break, Koo, her flatmate Liz Salamon, Prince Andrew and friends John Rickatson Hatt and Jocelyn Grey went along to see the smash hit musical *The Pirates of Penzance* in Drury Lane. Andrew, realising that he might be spotted, asked Liz to accompany him to the car and so keep Koo's identity secret. Koo readily agreed and even gave Liz her distinctive designer's coat to try and fool any waiting photographers. Koo held back while Andrew left and sure enough Andrew was photographed. Andrew's little ruse had Fleet Street buzzing with speculation. Some thought it was his former girlfriend Kim Deas, others guessed that it was Koo. They were all wide of the mark. The *Pirates* party was also the party that ended up flying to Mustique on board a British Airways Jumbo jet.

As Koo and Andrew walked on board under the names Mr and Mrs Cambridge they thought they has thrown the Press off the scent. But then Lady Luck decided to take a hand. By sheer chance *Daily Express* photographer Steve Wood and his nurse girlfriend Katie Hobbs were on the jet bound for a similar romantic holiday in the sun. During the flight Wood asked the British Airways steward if his girlfriend could go up to the flight deck.

He presented his business card, hoping that it would carry some weight. The steward, smelling a rat, promptly told Andrew's private detective that there was a Pressman on board. So Wood was astonished when he was approached by

Inspector Geoffrey Padgham, Andrew's burly bodyguard. 'You're not taking any pictures,' Padgham told him. Wood said afterwards: 'I thought he was talking about Princess Margaret. I didn't have a clue that Andrew was on the flight.' So he sauntered down the passenger isles keeping a sharp look out for Margaret. He even walked by Andrew without noticing him as he was looking for a woman. It was only when Katie spotted the Prince that the chase was on, but by this time he had taken himself up to the flight deck and watched as the Jumbo was landed at Antigua. Koo had also gone undercover, hiding herself under an airline blanket. Round one to Andrew – but by now the cat was well and truly out of the bag.

What started as a get away from it all holiday was to make headlines from Hong Kong to Heckmondwike. At the height of interest it was said that Government Ministers couldn't venture abroad without first being briefed on the latest on the Koo Stark affair. For they knew their foreign hosts were eager to hear up to the minute reports. As Andrew and friends climbed aboard a twin engined plane to take them on the last leg of their journey to Mustique little did they realise the interest they would generate. Certainly the island is an ideal place for a romantic holiday. Palm fringed beaches, clear warm waters, abundant tropical fish and powder blue skies make this four square mile island a picture postcard paradise. More than that discretion and privacy are guaranteed as the island is privately owned by the Mustique Company. Visitors must have somewhere to stay or they are thrown off at dusk as vagrants.

The Honourable Colin Tennant first put the island on the map when he asked Princess Margaret what she would like as a wedding gift. 'Would you like a bit of my island or something I can wrap up and send you,' he asked. Her acceptance of a six acre plot overlooking Lagoon Bay in the south of the island soon set house prices soaring. Rock star Mick Jagger has a wood built hideaway overlooking the half sunken wreck of the French passenger liner *Antilles* which steamed on to the reef just off the island in 1971. The island has had other famous visitors over the years – Racquel Welch, Lord Lichfield – who is Margaret's next-door neighbour – former Harrods' chairman Hugh Fraser and the Duke and Duchess of Kent. Even rock poet Bob Dylan has travelled to enjoy the peace and seclusion of an island where goats and chickens roam free and where the odd monkey is kept as a pet.

Margaret's cream coloured, plantation style holiday home overlooks a sandy bay some eighty feet or so above the sea. Koo and Andrew were able to reach the sea for early morning swims by negotiating two steep flights of stone steps cut into the rock. The interior of the house, designed by Margaret, is somewhat stark. In the drawing room she has a large portrait of her big sister hanging on the wall. 'It's so that people from abroad can see it's an English house,' she tells visitors. Indeed the island does have a very English flavour. The main street is called Royal Avenue and the largest bay is called Britannia Bay.

Margaret's villa first became well-known when she brought her boyfriend Roddy Llewellyn for a holiday during the early days of their friendship.

Roddy, now a full-time landscape gardener, designed the gardens for the house. And he had in mind not just creating a pretty effect when he planted a host of shrubs and bushes. It was also to fully screen the house and swimming pool from prying eyes below. A fact that proved a frustrating obstacle for the photographers waiting to picture Koo and Andy by the poolside.

It was into this relaxed, *laissez faire* atmosphere that Koo and company arrived. After they had taxied up the runway to the wooden Customs shed they were met by a blue Land Rover and driven the three miles to Jolies Eaux. On the way they passed Basil's Bar, the island's only restaurant and source of entertainment. Every week it stages a 'Jump Up' where a steel band plays under clear Caribbean skies. It was to become the headquarters and command centre for the Press operations that week.

While Koo and Andy swam and lazed by the villa's swimming pool, 8,000 miles away Koo's flat was under seige. Her Spanish-born cleaning lady Maria Rodriguez was gaily telling reporters about how she would save the mail for Koo and keep and eagle eye out for letters from Andrew and rush downstairs to Koo who would 'squeal with delight' when she received them. She added: 'I saw the Principe (Spanish for Prince) leave two or three times at about nine in the morning. He always looked rather tired.' It was a remark which collected her a place in the 'Quotes of the Year' – but several days later she also collected her cards. Even the normally po-faced BBC joined in the excitement, showing a scene from 'Emily' in their main news. That rush of blood to the head was quickly reprimanded by Tory MP Jack Aspinall.

But for Koo it could all be taking place a million miles away as she and Andrew gazed up at the stars and Andrew pointed out the Southern Cross, a star configuration that shines brightly over the nearby island of Becquia. It was a star formation he learned well during his days in the Falklands.

Their lazy days on holiday started with breakfast on the veranda. Andrew, an early riser, usually roused the others before they went for a typically tropical breakfast of pineapple, mangoes and guava watching the breakers roll up on the secluded beach below.

News of their arrival had the hearts of the local girls beating just a little faster. 'We're all jealous of Koo,' said one island worker. Another added: 'He's a lot better looking than Prince Charles. He's a real hero round here since the Falklands.' He was such a hit with the locals that the steel band composed a tune, The Randy Andy Mambo, in his honour. Andrew demonstrated his naturalness when the party went for a picnic on Macaroni Beach, a secluded bay where birds of paradise and love birds can be spotted. A local boatman Peter Jordan walked by the group as they sat under a palm roofed shelter. Andrew called him over and chatted to him about his life at sea. Then he invited the open-mouthed boatman to join them for their picnic lunch of cold chicken and sandwiches. Like dozens of others before him Peter came to the conclusion: 'Andrew didn't seem like a Prince at all.' But this open handed attitude was not to last. For with the arrival of reporters – including myself – and photographers from New York and London on board a small flotilla of yachts, Andrew and party kept near to the house or took a speedboat off the island entirely.

The Press had come for pictures of Koo and Andrew, hopefully on the beach, preferably hand in hand. It was not to be.

For once Andrew, the king of hearts, held all the aces. The Princess Margaret Set froze out the Press and the Mustique Company did everything they could to keep the photographers at bay. They banned the island's three taxis from carrying journalists, cut off the island's phones to the outside world and stopped newsmen from going anywhere but the tarmac road to the airport or the public beaches. While photographers trudged around the island on Shank's pony, Andy and Koo were able to drive the Land Rover, easily losing anyone in the labyrinth of dirt roads. He was dubbed a Prisoner In Paradise but his detective, Inspector Padgham, later admitted: 'Andrew wanted privacy and he got it. He managed to get around the island far more than you think.' Round Two to Andrew.

But the photographers weren't to be outdone so easily. Some crawled through the prickly thorn bushes to try get near the villa, others lay for hours in undergrowth near the beach. As they waited they had cause to recall that the island's name, Mustique, derives from the French for mosquito, a pest which thrives in the torrential showers and average 78°F heat. But even though no-one managed to get through Andrew's defence – he even helped in the look-out by using a pair of high powered binoculars – his bodyguard wasn't satisfied.

He drafted in a plane load of extra police from

the nearby island of St Vincent. They were stationed around the house and patrolled the beaches. Private security guards also helped in the elaborate game of hide and seek that could have come straight from the pages of Boys' Own Paper. Each morning at 4am, the silence would be broken by the sound of small outboard motors ferrying photographers ashore. They would creep onto the island and spend several hours blundering about in the pitch dark looking for a likely spot where Andrew might appear. On one occasion a freelance photographer from New York got so close to the house that he overheard Inspector Padgham briefing his men. 'Be on your guard,' he told them. 'These Fleet Street types will stop at nothing to get the story.' The local five strong police force were somewhat bemused by these antics. The worst crime on their books was to find the villain who poisoned a woman resident's pet dog. She was offering 500 Caribbean dollars for information about the culprit. So when the brown shirted private security guards started holding photographers at pistol point they decided to withold their co-operation from an episode which could easily have turned from farce to tragedy. Even when two freelance photographers were arrested in the grounds of Princess Margaret's villa the episode went from the absurd to the ridiculous. It fully warranted a mention in Evelyn Waugh's comic book about journalism called *Scoop*.

They were taken to the island's only cell, a tiny bare room, right next door to the local church. All afternoon they listened to gospel songs belted out by a local temperance religious sect. Before they were arrested they managed to take a shot of Andrew on the balcony looking out to sea. It was the only picture to emerge from the week long siege. While they were in jail they had the consolation of being served a lobster lunch by concerned colleagues. As news of their arrest filtered back, the telephone lines from Melbourne, New York and London were glowing red hot to the local police station. The harassed station sergeant, chickens running round his feet, was almost in tears as he tried to placate angry editors and lawyers. Eventually the men were released with a warning. If the pace on the sleepy island was hotting up, in London it had reached boiling point. Screaming headlines said that an 'angry' Queen who was touring Australia with Prince Philip, had ordered Andrew home. But Buckingham Palace soon put the record straight, stating calmly that Andrew was a 22-year-old helicopter pilot and that spoke for itself. They added revealingly: 'It would be his choice and judgement, and that would never be questioned by the Queen.' As one royal observer noted: 'The very idea of the Queen being angry or in a rage is unthinkable.'

The incident does show how the Queen and Prince Philip treat their children. It is with a mixture of good humour and common sense, not stiff formality and rigid codes of conduct as may have been the case a century ago. Prince Charles once said that his parents were not the sort of people who lay down the law but at the same time nor are they the type who let their offspring do just as they like. They encourage them to develop their own interests and personality and yet stay an integral part of the family. For family life is sacred to the

Queen. It was neatly summed up by Princess Anne who once said: 'The greatest advantage of my entire life is the family I grew up in. The family was always there, the feeling of being in a family and we are the stronger for it.'

Queen Victoria's acid comment about her own son's children: 'Such ill-bred, ill-trained children. I cannot fancy any of them,' could certainly not be applied to the Queen's family.

If Fleet Street was getting into a lather about Andrew's antics he wasn't letting it bother him. He neatly evaded the Press by chartering a speedboat and taking Koo to the nearby islands of Tobago Keys. They spent the day snorkelling and examining the exotic species of fish on this coral reef. And he showed how easy it was to outwit the world's Press when he drove by the bar where they drowned their sorrows. While one American journalist was desperately discussing the possibility of hiring a helicopter to try and winkle out the Prince, he was yards away disguised in a floppy hat and sunglasses and carrying an armful of groceries. Andrew has been well trained in the art of shaking off newshounds by Charles. He has a list of tricks 'as long as your arm' to use to shake off newsmen. One of the tricks was stopping reporters using the island's phones. Instead they had to resort to their ship to shore radios. One message shouted over the ship's radio to the patient telex operator in St Vincent could have gone drastically wrong. When the reporter shouted out: 'Prince Andrew cocked a snook at world opinion yesterday,' it was so badly scrambled that the telex operator read back: 'Prince Andrew caught a snoek fish yesterday.' Such are the hazards of royal reporting!

The fact that Andrew's holiday was the talk of dinner tables around the world did not put him off his stride. He was up to his well known practical jokes. One day he took personal delivery of some fresh lobsters for supper that night. With one clutched in each hand he crept up on Koo while she was sunbathing by the pool. As she squealed in mock terror he tried to shove one down her bikini, a 'claws' encounter that had the whole party laughing. But like all good things the holiday had to come to an end. Some folk said that he cut short his holiday because of Press pestering but he had always planned to go on the day that he departed. But not in quite such a dramatic fashion. Koo and friends outfoxed the Press and took an early morning plane to St Lucia, then on to Miami and into hiding.

Andrew's departure proved to be much more hair raising. HRH Andrew turned into His Royal Hijacker when he took the plane I had chartered for my colleague, *Daily Star* photographer Ken Lennox. It was a fitting climax to a week of hide and seek. The pilot was due to pick up Lennox and fly him to St Vincent so that he could make his connection to Barbados and so home to Heathrow. As he walked towards the plane clutching his baggage, the pilot roared off down the runway. A Land Rover came from nowhere out of the bushes and drove to Lennox's plane. Another photographer gave chase but he was grabbed by a gun-toting security guard and a bloody fight ensued.

Meanwhile the Prince, wearing his disguise of a floppy hat and sunglasses, passed the scuffle and ran for the plane. The pilot opened up the throttle and headed straight for Lennox who was standing by the side of the runway. He said afterwards: 'I threw myself to the ground a fraction of a second before the wing passed over me. I felt the draught of the propellor as I hugged the ground. I was terrified.' He was left stranded, but not for long. He caught up with me in Barbados and we sat behind the Prince in the first class section of the British Airways flight to Heathrow.

With a grin Prince Andrew turned to me and said: 'Good evening Mr Morton, how are you?' That twinkle in his eyes said that it was honours even for the last round in the amazing duel between Press and Prince. He chatted during the flight and was obviously in good spirits. And he had time to remember Koo, buying her a huge bottle of Chanel N° 5, her favourite perfume. As we flew over Lands End he gazed eagerly down to see if he could spot Culdrose airbase where he was soon to report for duty. Back home and back in uniform he had some good news when he reported for duty at 820 helicopter squadron. His hours of flying experience in the Falklands had earned him promotion. He was upgraded from a helicopter co-pilot to a full pilot. It means he now has full responsibility for the huge Sea King when he takes it on operations, however hazardous. Within the next couple of years he will be promoted from a Sublieutenant to full Lieutenant, an elevation that should come early because of his Falklands experience.

When he arrived back at Culdrose he had to endure some playful rubbings from his colleagues about his Mustique holiday. But he took it all in good part. Princess Margaret said soon afterwards: 'Andrew said he had an absolutely smashing time on Mustique. He had a lovely holiday.' More painful perhaps was the fact that one of the party, Liz Salamon, was busily touting round her 'exclusive' revelations about the holiday for a sum rumoured at £100,000. Before they left the island Andrew tried to nip any future problems in the bud by offering to develop the films the party took.

In spite of the intense publicity surrounding the affair Koo and Andrew still see each other. They spent the weekend at Floors Castle in Scotland as guests of Andrew's friend, the Duke of Roxburghe. While Andrew went hunting, Koo took the Duke's dog for a walk.

But speculation that the couple would spend New Year together at Sandringham with the rest of the royal family proved somewhat wide of the mark. Instead Koo splashed out £170 for a sky-blue skiing outfit and spent the New Year on the slopes at fashionable St Moritz.

Before she left, the nation was left on tenterhooks by the royal romance. For Koo was spotted making an evening visit to Andrew at his rooms at Buckingham Palace just before Christmas. Days later she was spotted and approached by housewife Eileen Paxton in Kensington High Street just after Koo had finished her ski shopping.

Eileen, who told Koo: 'Marry Andrew and to hell with the consequences,' was delighted when the love-lorn young woman told her that she indeed loved Andrew and he loved her. Where will it all end?

In November the traditional Remembrance Day service took on special significance as the nation remembered the 256 men who gave their lives and the hundreds of others who were scarred in the battle for the Falklands. When Andrew asked his mother to lay a wreath at the Cenotaph ceremony she was delighted to give her approval. On a wet and dull Sunday watched by ambassadors, Ministers and millions more glued to their TV sets he marched smartly forward and gently laid his wreath besides those of his mother, Prince Philip and Prince Charles. Then he took four paces back and gave a stiff, lingering salute. It was a poignant moment. Observers couldn't make up their minds whether it was the chill November rain or tears which ran down his cheeks as he stood in silence, remembering. More than anyone Andrew, with his youth, exuberance and striking good looks, symbolised the young men who fought so valiantly 8,000 miles away.

His part in the struggle has earned him high praise from those who six months earlier were saying: 'Isn't it time that Andrew grew up?' By his own actions he had answered questions about his maturity and sense of responsibility. He had modestly recounted his own actions in the war, remembering his moments of high drama when death was a Sea Wolf missile locked onto the belly of his Sea King or an Exocet heading towards *Invincible*. Like thousands of others he was simply doing his job but he proved beyond question that he was not simply a playboy Prince but a warrior who has truly earned his wings.

Whither Andrew? The Navy lark will be Andrew's life at least until he is thirty and Service chiefs see no reason why he should not continue for a much longer period. Like his father before him, Andrew is a career Naval officer and he will hope to progress steadily through the ranks of the Senior Service. It is a long established royal tradition for the younger sons to go into the Service, and if Andrew shows himself to be a real high flier he could well make the rank of commander by his early thirties. Before that he will face the choice between sea and land . . . continuing flying in the front line as a submarine hunter with Sea King helicopters staying on station and teaching younger pilots the tricks of his trade, or joining the glamour boys flying the 'racing cars of the sky' – the speedy 2-man Lynx helicopters. No doubt his sights will be set on reaching the same seniority as his father and commanding his own ship.

When he marries – be it to Koo or another – his Civil List pay will more than double from £20,000 to £50,000 a year. It is virtually certain that he will be made the Duke of York, a traditional honour bestowed on the monarch's younger sons. Indeed in the last 500 years there have only been three exceptions to this pattern.

In many respects he is a very fortunate young man. As a result of his naval commitments he is spared many of the tedious but essential royal duties. The endless round of inspections, receptions and openings will never be his lot. In any case he would resent being the third fiddle in the royal orchestra. So, as with his appearance at the opening of the Regent Street lights, he is able to pick and choose his engagements, flitting in and out of the limelight at will. But one thing is certain, the playboy Prince will never be far from the headlines. For in Andrew the royals have found a young man with star quality.

THE END